FROM RUFIO
TO ZUKO

Dante Basco

Basco, Dante

ISBN: 978-1-945649-36-3
Fire Nation edition

ISBN: 978-1-945649-35-6
Lost Boys edition

Edited by Safia Elhillo and Rhiannon McGavin
Cover design by Cassidy Trier
Editorial design by Ian DeLucca
Proofread by Rhiannon McGavin

Not a Cult
Los Angeles, CA

Printed in Canada

CONTENTS

INTRODUCTION

Denver Airport 6:06am

I'm up, didn't sleep at all last night; it's been three weekends
in a row now that I've been out of town. On the road, in places
I never knew existed until the very moment I wound up there.
Then here. Denver, Colorado. ComicCon all weekend (no sleep)
and a Monday morning flight so early that the car picked me
up at 4:30 a.m. I worried I might oversleep, and that anxiety
kept me wired. Now, here I am. Middle of the country. Before
the sunrise, but in an airport I know quite well. In my career
you zig-zag, and my zig-zags often leave me in limbo here. I
grab the same bagel at that one eatery they have in every ter-
minal, then I hit up the same store for "essentials." It's not even
really a store so much as an enclosed kiosk that sells outdoor
jackets. You can't go outdoors at the Denver Airport and I'm
usually bouncing between significantly warmer cities. Regardless, I wind up buying jackets. I have too many jackets already.
There's a slight concern that I have a jacket addiction. Maybe
you'll understand it? They seem substantial to me in some way
and perhaps I have a deep-seeded fear of being cold. Does that
count as a metaphor?

I'm writing a book about my life. It's going very well so far, as I assume you can tell. This might wind up scattered. Primarily because I don't think I should be writing a book. I'm only 42 years young. Is that old enough to be worthy of a book? Is that perhaps too old to be writing a book at this point? Does anyone want to read what I have to say? You're here right now, but are you sure that you'll see this through to the end? I don't know if I can.

I'm writing a book and it's going very well so far.

We ended things— me and the woman I've been in a relationship with for eleven years. We ended it, and it went down heavy. It's still heavy. This isn't denial, but I'm doing my best not to think about it. I haven't written about it yet, not for myself or anyone else. As much as I want to keep these feelings wrapped until they heal a bit more, it's like I'm bleeding through the bandages. It's all around me. I thought I could do this travel, and abandon this hurt at home. I can almost hear your eyes roll. You're not wrong. You can't leave a memory like a place. It's a curse that will linger in the air wherever you go. It lives in your breath.

I don't really know what to do about emotional hauntings, so my best bet is to dive in. Put words on the page. Accept what I cannot control and exorcise the rest onto the infinite canvas of a digital page. Truly lose myself in the foreverness of a void.

I'm writing a book and it's going very well so far.

Hey. The sun is rising in Denver, and we'll be lining up to board soon. I can escape this airport, this exhaustion, but not the baggage I'm bringing with me. Not my carry-on; but rather the… oh, you get it. I was trying to be clever but, again, no sleep and too many thoughts. You understand. Now I'm thinking about what I'll be returning to in Los Angeles. I'll collapse onto my bed. That part I'm looking forward to. I'll need to clean my house. When you live your life on the road, sometimes your apartment devolves into less of a habitat and more of a slightly welcoming closet. A storage unit for myself and the Dante-adjacent accessories. Then I have to talk to my accountant. God, will that come before the sweet embrace of my mattress? I have to file income taxes for myself. I have to file separate income taxes for my businesses. I worry that I've become a grown-up. A grown-up who pays multiple sets of taxes. It's an odd aspect of adulthood to fixate on, but I feel like I should be more coherent about this. One clear feeling. That's not coming. With bonafide maturity, does this happen more often? Does everything start to blur? Or does this emotional smudge feel exaggerated because of my identity? The world knows me, first and foremost, as a child actor. An entire generation grew up watching me grow up, whether they knew it or not. Would my transition into— I don't know, what phase of life is 42? Does my transition into this period represent a difficult growth, not only for me, but collectively, for everyone who shared in my upbringing?

It is possible that I'm too tired to be starting this right now. Does this all track? You still with me? Thanks for your patience. I think this is all going somewhere.

The world knows me as a child actor. And it always will. That was where we started, and I won't be able to change that. I used to fight against this. I've found a peace with it. I think. I hope. As a child actor, I was one of the only Asian American kids that appeared on film, from the mid-'80s through most of the '90s. On into the 2000s. I still work today, but I remain frozen for most people. In their mind, I will always be the person I was at that very specific point. Even now, in my 40s, I voice teenage characters in animated productions. A director once told me that I was "timeless." It's certainly a compliment, but it's a complicated compliment.

Even if I wanted to struggle against my career's cryogenic state, I would have to battle the most iconic character of my career. In the film *Hook*, I played the role of Rufio. He was the leader of The Lost Boys. And The Lost Boys never grew up. I'm not a child infused with the magic of an imaginary land. I grew up. But I am still, literally, a lost boy.

Definitely lost right now.

I'm writing a book and maybe this isn't the right time.

If you're going to come with me on this adventure, as you've probably come with me on adventures before, I want you to have some concept of where we're going. I surely don't have life's big answers, and I doubt that I know more than anyone else about any particular subject. I don't even have the benefit of time, since I'm just dipping a toe into "middle-aged." Old enough to be just a bit depressing, but not old enough to wax poetic with any degree of accuracy. Crap.

So my plan is to look back at my own adventure. And the story doesn't belong to me alone. I have a family full of important figures that helped shape who I've become. Who continue to shape where I will go. They're the co-authors here.

In a bigger picture, this isn't even our story. Much of this is about the Asian American experience in Hollywood. And what a childhood in that place can do to you. My family was recognized by the mayor of Los Angeles as the "First Major Asian American Entertainment Family." I still don't fully understand what that means, but I have some ideas. It means that we figured out how to pull off creative work in an oppressive environment, and other people might learn from our success. It also means that we have a responsibility in our community. My life has been spent trying to fulfill that responsibility. I hope I'm doing well in that regard. If nothing else, I believe I've paved roads for those that come after me.

I'm writing like I'm about to die. I'm 42. I'll try to be a bit less serious about this moving forward. Sorry, I'm feeling this whole thing out with you. I promise I'm not going to die before we're done.

Oh. Sun is up. Boarding soon. Gotta wrap this up.

I'm sharing my adventure from the beginning, because none of this means anything unless you see the context and influences that positioned me for these opportunities. Then I want to look at a career that has lasted for more than 20 years. There's a lot here that I haven't dedicated time toward, and we might both get something out of that. Worst case scenario: it'll have some wild stories. It is undeniably a unique story. But the elements can be replicated by you and your community, no matter where you are or what you're hoping to accomplish. Every word of this tale is about chasing a dream. I caught my dream. The odds were a million to one. I'd like to think that some detail I etch here will give you the edge you need to catch yours. We're all on the same team. Us against the universe.

I'm writing a book, and I hope we're outlining your book in the process.

GROWING UP BASCO

On January 5th, this'll be my 30th year in Hollywood. Yeah, so it's been a long time— it still sounds crazy. I've spent my whole career at the ground level in the entertainment industry. Do you know what the ground level of the entertainment industry is?

At least for me, it was the actual ground. Me and my brothers were street performers in San Francisco. B-boys, meaning break-boys, meaning us— we called ourselves the Street Freaks. We started our career battling other b-boy groups in the golden era of hip-hop, the '80s. Always considered myself, and still consider myself, a hip-hop artist. I went from dancing to music to filmmaking.

Of course, not only were we breakdancers, but we also had breakdancing names. My brothers were Klassical Kid, Dynamic Dar, Midget Master, and I was Pop n' Fresh. We all had our own specialty moves: I saw myself as someone who could do a bunch of different moves, but definitely had a killer head spin. It was the birth of hip-hop, and we were totally enraptured by it. We spent so much time breakdancing, or thinking about breakdancing. I remember nights falling asleep in the garage, turned into a makeshift dance studio on the wooden panel we placed on the ground. Wood panel was better than cardboard boxes, more slippery for all the spins and such. I remember actually sleeping on the panel, and waking up with a blanket my mom probably put on me during the night, and going into a back spin before getting up and getting breakfast.

We battled everybody. We did so many contests: my mother did the stats, and we won 32 breakdancing contests in total. We got so popular that we started getting picked up and paid to dance. We danced for the Oakland A's, the San Francisco 49ers, and even got scholarships to the San Francisco Ballet Company. That opened up a land of fine arts to us, of what dancing was beyond the culture of hip-hop.

We were a bunch of blue-collar kids from a blue-collar town outside San Francisco called Pittsburg. My dad was a telephone man, and my mom was our mother. She didn't have many opportunities growing up, and she wanted to give us all that she wished she'd had.

She gave us the world.

She kept us forever busy— to keep us out of trouble. From the dance classes to gymnastics, piano lessons, swim classes, forever driving us around in that maroon Chevy conversion van. I remember playing in the back with my brothers— in those days before seatbelt laws, we wrestled and got rowdy, just as you would expect from boys tumbling around the back of a van. To the point where my mom would yell at us to settle down. She would also yell out to help her change lanes on the freeways. We spent hours in that van when we were kids. Driving to and from San Francisco, stuck in traffic for hours. Mondays, Wednesdays and Fridays at the Ballet, piano and gymnastics in between.

My mom would wait in the car, reading a book, never complaining, just watching through the window.

Our parents weren't performers. They didn't really have any advice to offer us, so they simply offered support. I never knew if we were any good at the things we did. The other kids had parents that constantly reminded them that they were the best in the world. Our parents were always just happy that we had fun. I recognize today that this is what healthy support of a child *actually* looks like. But when you're in it as a kid, it's tricky to see that.

One day, my mother came to me and my brothers and said, "You guys want to take the leap and become little fish in the ocean of Hollywood?" I said yes, we all did, and we ended up moving to LA.

We jumped in our van with $100. My dad sent money as we went along, and gave us a year to make something happen. We took that trip to Hollywood, and I was ten years old. That's a full lifetime of events that I'd managed to squeeze in by age ten.

From ten on was Hollywood. They'd ask, "Where you from?"
"Where you from?"
Well, that's a loaded question.
See, I grew up in a blue-collar town
with the blacks and the browns
and me being in that category
plus my pops made less than 40
G's, yeah, it's clear to see me, well I can be
blue-collar
better yet broke most of the time
even better poor
but when you're young and you're poor,
you don't know that you're poor
never occurs to you that you don't have a bed everyone

sleeps on the floor
eighteen in a house, one bathroom, someone always
knocking on the door
At least it was fun.

Let's get back to the topic.
"Where are you from?"
See, where I'm from, there are cops and there are gangsters
also known as gangbangers
unlike the cops and robbers in the movies.
But unlike the movies, it's not so black-and-white.
There are areas of gray
that is to say
it's hard to distinguish the difference between
pulled over by a cop
and being hit up by a gangster. Let me explain.
Followed by a cop, followed six blocks
pulled over by a cop, he looks at you
and says
"WHERE ARE YOU FROM?"
He does not
wait for you to reply
he accuses you and you deny
you're from the eastside.
"No, sir"
Bow your head, don't look him in the eyes.
He pulls you out the car
you're sitting on the curb
it's embarrassing watching the cars drive by
but then you wonder if that's just another part of life.

Now, when it comes to the
gangbanger
all you got is to be a stranger

when he asks you
"Where you from?"
you can feel it laced with danger.
So watch what you say next because you're playing with danger.
Don't come to east
don't come to west
Matter fact, same rules apply:
bow your head, don't look him in the eyes.
"I ain't from nowhere, man, I'm just some guy."
See, he too
sees you
as a mark.
But they don't really see you
your face,
or your heart.
All they see
are marks.

Now, me being me,
I've got a few
tricks up my sleeve.
Messed up situations, I've gotten out of
few of those by simply
picking my nose.

That's right, picking my nose.

See, when a cop pulls up,
and I casually try to pick a booger from my nose
For a second, just a moment,
I'm exposed.
To be a man, not a mark
a human being just like you

you got boogers, too.
And the cop you see just continues to roll down the street
and the gangsters, they just laugh and leave.
See, when you see yourself in someone else
it could set you free.

The funny thing is, I'm probably from where they're from.
The other side of town,
I'm just trying to get home.

I am a poet. That's something most folks don't know about me. In 1998, I started a poetry venue in my living room, originally called Dante's Poetry Lounge. That became DPL, Da Poetry Lounge in L.A. It's now 23 years old.

I'm not trying to brag. Maybe I am. You know, just a little bit.

I find it incredibly difficult to be proud of my work. Not on the inside, which is where I think it matters most. I've spent my life working around people with enough hubris bubbling out of them at all times to know what an unsexy look that is. I never want to be like that. In fact, I never really want to be in the spotlight.

Yes, I can hear you from here. Maybe I chose the wrong career path for avoiding attention. I'm very aware, I promise.

My difficulty is that I can only see myself through the eyes of other people. I have a flaw in wanting to be liked. Maybe that's not the worst flaw in the world. Maybe that's a fault that absolutely every single one of us feels, and I just think my version of it is extra special. My friends would probably describe me as a "likable person." I come from a long line of very even-keeled men. I don't like to say no to people, and I try to do what is asked of me, and I try to never make a big deal out of it. I'm quiet, even in the moments that become the biggest for me.

My childhood is the source of all this.

Very few actors actually "make it" and even fewer earn a living. Mathematically, none of us should make it. When I give lectures at colleges now, I ask everyone to look at the person to their left and then the person to their right. Then I say, none of you will make it. You just aren't. It's like medical school or law school but to the nth degree. Having even the smallest blip of a Hollywood career is as likely as this laptop turning into gold as I type, or me walking into the kitchen and figuring out how to divide by zero.

So coming up Asian American was already pushing those numbers even harder against me. I'm not even the "normal" Asian American. I'm southeast Asian. And I survived in the hardest industry in the world for thirty years. And flourished. My million-to-one shot was a ten-million-to-one shot. And I did it. How do you take a similar shot? How did I pull this together?

When can I take a step back from this and be proud in the way I deserve?

Well. That's complicated.

I was ten years old when I got to LA with my brothers. And it was the first time I really understood ethnicity, or who I was as a Filipino. We trusted in the inalienable rights we had as Americans. You can't be hired or fired from any job based on your gender or ethnicity or religion. That's all basic knowledge, right? Or at least it's supposed to work that way.

When you come to Hollywood, you understand that they are hiring you precisely on what you look like. Being Filipino American, there have only been fragments of roles in the last thirty years. They just aren't there. Just as history is written by the victors, the life experiences written by the folks at the top of the food chain in Hollywood are the stories that white, straight men have lived. Or can see themselves relating to. Diversity can only come from the top-down, and that's a glacial battle.

Despite this, I've been able to not just succeed, but flourish and prosper in that industry. How does one flourish in a famished situation?

I would walk into a room, and in the '80s they'd just ask "Well, what are you?"

Well, what are you?

"I'm Filipino." They'd ask straight-up, "What is that?" As a kid, I realized quickly how to adapt. As a kid, I realized that my identity mattered less than getting the work. My identity was malleable. My identity, over time, becomes mist.

This role is for a Chinese character. I wouldn't straight out lie about taking any other race. I'd sell it much better than that. "Well, my grandmother on my Dad's side...she's part Chinese." Which is actually true. That kind of answer was always good enough. Any amount of anything meant I was all of that thing, in the eyes of a casting director. They'd checked their box. They found a "Chinese" actor. They'd done their job and I grew up understanding the reciprocal role I would play in this dance.

My grandmother on my Dad's side is part Chinese. Now I'm Chinese. Now I've got the gig.

It could get more granular. I got better at this as time went on. They'd explain that the role was for a "Mexican" and then ask...

Well, what are you?

I'd stand up a little straighter. "Well, you understand when the Spanish colonized Mexico, they colonized us the same in the Philippines, so we're Latino also."

Any amount of anything meant I was all of that thing, in the eyes of a casting director. They'd checked their box. They found a "Mexican" actor. Now I've got the gig. And they got a free lesson in imperialism mid-talent search.

This turned into me being able to book all kinds of roles, but never Filipino. Playing Mexican roles, Puerto Rican roles, Chinese, Korean, every Asian role. Never playing any Filipino roles until I did *The Debut*.

If no race was specified on a casting call, that just meant white. I booked those too— I beat a lot white kids out for Rufio. Whether it was a white role or Black role, I was always the other choice at the final audition. If you're a person of color, and you're not beating the white kids out of "their" jobs every once in awhile, the casting directors aren't really seeing you. The star quality in you. They're only focused on the surface.

But during that time, amazing things started to happen. I was working as a child actor, and I got a big break. I was discovered by Steven Spielberg for this multicultural group of misfit kids, and their leader was...me. This Filipino, red tri-hawked, hip-hop kid. People come up to me to this day like, "Yo, you were the first cool Asian character I ever saw on television." Interracial couples come to me like, "Yo man. Growing up, my girl, my wife? She had a big crush on you. I know for sure that you are one of the reasons why she married me."

Well, what are you?

You'd think I would know by now. I ask myself often enough.

The answer always changes but a few pillars remain standing.

Before we move into the glamorous and gritty Hollywood tales, and my adventures in getting murdered by Captain Hook (spoilers!), I'd like to tell you a little bit more about who my family is. I want you to know who they are when they get mentioned again and again throughout my story, because of course, they are my story. Also, I think if I wrote a book without giving them credit for what they've given me, they'd probably beat me up.

I'm joking.

I think?

Nah. I'd be fine. This is just important to put in.

As you may have noticed, I'm Filipino. Did I mention that before? That's going to come up more often throughout. Sorry in advance, but it's kindaaaaa important to what I do. Filipino Americans also call themselves Fil-Ams. My parents are from the Philippines— they were both born there, as were my grandparents. My dad was actually born an American citizen, because my grandfather was a World War II veteran and war hero. He was an officer in the army, and that's how they immigrated to the U.S. My mother's father also served the U.S., but in the Navy. That's ultimately how my mom's side immigrated here.

I wasn't here for all that. I was here for 152 Regent Drive in Pittsburg, California.

Filipinos are family. Where you're from should be part of your last name, because especially if you're from Pittsburg, CA? We're probably related. Whether by blood or water. Anyone older than you was your uncle or aunt, the ones older than them were extra grandparents, everyone else was your cousin. There are family names that are prevalent in town, like my own, the Bascos, or the Nazarettas or Gusimats or Bomagats... but in a lot of ways, Pittsburg is our last name too, an experience we all shared.

The house I grew up in, the first place I can remember, was in a part of town called Buchanan. This was a two-story house. Tract homes, but I felt it still had its charm. I lived there with my mom, dad, my brothers and sister. And like many immigrant families, my grandparents also lived with us— my dad's parents, Grandpa and Grandma Basco.

This house was the center of the universe, the stage of a larger story that spanned a century. The place where all of my family would commune— not just my immediate family, but my uncles and aunts, of whom I had more than a few. My dad is one of seven children, and my mom is one of six. All of my cousins would come through and beyond that, my mom ran a daycare for the neighborhood kids, who would be racing cars between tea parties late into the night. The house rang with the joyous noise of people at all hours. The bustle of conversation would wake me up every morning, and I'd stumble to the kitchen curious about what was being cooked, and more curious about the gossip.

This house always held a sort of magic to me. My family bought this house before it was even built. We would go see it being constructed, playing around on the lot of land while my grandma threw coins into the foundation as the cement was being poured. She said it would bring us good luck.

This house is where we started our whole life in entertainment. I say us because I'm talking about me and my brothers: Derek, Darion, and Dion. Arianna, our sister, would later follow in our footsteps, and dance and act and write poetry. But it truly began in the living room of that house, where we would dance and perform for the family and friends that came through, and where we'd stay up until dawn rehearsing for breakdancing competitions. Being Filipino, I think we all did that... sing and dance. I have incredible memories of my parents cha cha-ing in the living room, a chorus of my aunts and uncles singing. Mostly stuff from the 70's and 80's, anything from Smokey Robinson to the Eagles, usually one or two people on guitars. And everybody dancing.

Performing in front of bigger crowds started at the Fil-Am, the Filipino American Association. It's a place where a bunch of folks got together for parties and meetings, kinda like a Sportsmen's Lodge. My dad was the Vice President, and my grandfather had been the president when I was younger. Looking at the wall of past presidents and reading my family name up there made me proud. It still does. See, this is a place that raised me and my brothers and so many others. There were so many parties throughout the year— all of our parents knew each other, and us kids had our own scene, just running around and having fun.

The Fil-Am community had these big family events, from amusement park trips and skiing in Tahoe, to summer barbecues where it seemed like all the Filipinos in America would show up for food and games. The biggest event of the year, the Christmas party, always had a talent show for the local kids.

It's my first memory of being on a stage. I performed "Greased Lightning" for the show with my brothers Darion and Dion. *Grease* was one of my favorite movies, and I often credit that film, and John Travolta in particular, as part of why I wanted to become an actor. My mom made our outfits: velvet Grease vests with red silk lining. I must have been seven years old, or even younger, when we did this routine. We watched the movie dozens of times and knew the choreography pretty well, but we didn't quite understand all the content in the lyrics— the song is all about sex, and full of swear words. But we performed it, and I remember how electric it felt. Throughout my life, performing on stage still generated that shock.

From there, we were a staple of the Christmas show, with performances ranging from traditional dancing to magic acts to karate demonstrations. Then hip-hop swept the country, and I was enamored by the whole thing, the fashion and the music and the dancing... breakdancing. Dance became my first love.

There was Travolta combing his hair back to the beat in *Grease,* or gliding across the technicolor disco floor of *Saturday Night Fever.* The whole world clapped for the greatest dancer of all when Michael Jackson came on the scene with "Billie Jean"— he was a big influence on me as a young dancer. But before him, believe it or not, Travolta was the greatest dancer in my eyes. We would watch *Dance Fever,* hosted by Danny Terrio, because he was known to us as the guy who taught Travolta how to dance. In my household, like many Filipino households, dancing was forever part of family parties, mostly partner dancing. I loved seeing my parents cha-cha at parties. I still love seeing them dance together; they're both so smooth, always in tune with each other. When they dance, it's clear as a diamond from a chandelier: they are so, so in love. Maybe that's the real reason why I fell in love with dancing myself.

I've always considered my mother Aida as the dreamer to my father's realism. She always had so much energy, enough to put us on her back and carry us through the day. My mother was the torch that guided us with this incredible positivity that oozed from her, and made us feel like any journey was possible. I've always been amazed by her energy. My whole life, she's been up working before I woke, and after I went to bed. A giver almost to a fault, she's the heart and soul of our family. She'd give anyone absolutely all that she has. As a matter of fact, any time I've gifted her something "nice" or expensive, she'd give it away. Although she never bothered much with material things in the first place— she focused with saintlike care on her kids, the lives we would lead, the happiness we could craft from the world around us.

My whole career was really dependent on my mother's willingness to support my goals as a child actor. Who do you think drove me around town? We would spend hours together in the van. She'd ask how the audition went— sometimes I would ignore her, or pretend I was sleeping. I don't know why I was such a little asshole. Sometimes I didn't think she'd understand, or maybe I just didn't want to talk about it. As kids, sometimes we don't realize that the dreams we chase might grow from the hopes of our parents.

She often told us that her childhood had been less than bright, and one of her goals with her own family was to give us all the things that she didn't have growing up. And she did: from the shiny floors of dance studios to martial arts uniforms. Balance beams in gymnastics class and the sparkling water of swim lessons.

There were always so many activities for my brothers and me, and any of our cousins who happened to be around. We'd pile into the family van in a way that would most definitely be illegal these days, with nearly twenty kids in nine seats and no seatbelts in sight. And my mom at the wheel, taking our motley crew to the day's next activity.

Our house was where everyone else sent their troubled kids to help get straightened out. Between my mother and father, there was some special touch they had in raising their own kids, and they somehow had the same magic to give to our cousins, or distant relatives, or other kids from the neighborhood. My dad kept a few pairs of boxing gloves in the house, reserved for us boys. When there were disagreements, we had to put on those classic, red leather gloves, and just duke it out. You know how toxic masculinity becomes... problem-solving masculinity? That was this situation.

In so many ways, my dad was born to be a father. His name is Darius, although nobody ever calls him that. We called him Dad or Pops, and his grandkids call him Poppa. My whole life, I've heard his friends and family call him Day-O, like the Harry Belafonte song...*Daylight come and it's time to go home.* I always loved that name, always thought it was cool. What can I say about my dad? Only that he may be one of the best men I've ever known. I look at him now and he stands 5'6, but he's a giant in my eyes forever.

As for me and my brothers, it's hard to overstate how close we are. We studied together for so long in the same acting class, and performed in our breakdancing group even before that! It's like a kung fu movie— each brother develops different skills, different styles that somehow complements the rest of the crew. Sometimes that's good, and sometimes we're not encouraged to be full people, or artists, because we're part of a bigger team. It's just how it was with the brothers.

My oldest brother Derek is five years older than me, to the day. We're both born on August 29th, and it's been said that I was his best birthday present ever. As the oldest, he became the babysitter for me and my brothers and sister growing up. In a lot of ways, he was the perfect older brother. He was the oldest boy of all the cousins too; between that, his good grades, and his piano skills, he was the family favorite. When we moved to Los Angeles to follow our dreams, my father stayed in the Bay Area for a few years and sent money down, as he hadn't gotten a job transfer yet. Derek became our father figure in the household. I can't imagine all the pressure he felt, growing up as the eldest. I think of his strength perhaps more than anything else now, reflecting on our childhood.

Darion's the second oldest son in the family. He's been my best friend since I was born.

We're only 18 months apart, and people mistook us for twins growing up. So we've always been close, but still so different. I mean, he's arguably the best-looking of the brothers, angular and whatnot, as according to Derek. Definitely the most athletic in the bunch. I remember him touching the basketball rim when we were still in junior high. He was the kind of guy that made you feel, when he was on your team, that you had a good chance of winning. When we were on the same team in almost anything— basketball, trivia pursuit, whatever— we usually won...especially if Dion was on the other team. He's the youngest brother and that's just how things work out sometimes for younger brothers.

But Dion, Dion's always been my funniest brother. Dionysio, the smallest of the brothers in age and size. I often tease him and say he's the runt of the family, but he really is amazing. He's always been my little brother, even now in our forties. I sometimes still introduce him like that— probably isn't fair to him. He's like all of our friends' little brother in a way. But you should never underestimate the little brother, he'll surprise you.

With Arianna, the absolute youngest in the family, the mold broke and all the rules changed. Now, being the only girl in a household of boys running rampant, she has a love/hate relationship with the rest of us. Mostly love. I hope? I hope. Mostly love. Let's stick to that.

She was the classic kid sister. I remember seeing her in the wings when my brothers and I performed with our breakdancing crew in front of audiences. She knew all of our routines, dancing in unison with us center stage. My mom made her costumes that matched ours— she was our little sister, I knew she looked up to us, but because she was so much younger than us brothers, and she was a girl, she was never really part of the breakdancing crew.

That's where some of the hate comes in... well, not hate, maybe that's too strong of a word, but definitely tension, tension in a way that sometimes she feels we don't take her seriously, or she's not one of the boys, part of the group. She was not part of the breakdancing group in the '80s when we were coming up, she was not part of the rap band all us brothers were in called Fly Brown Dragons in the '90s. Arianna was part of the acting class that shaped us, but ended up leaving before we did. She saw the toxicity in the class before me and the brothers did. At the time, we blamed her for falling in love, but she just knew before we did.

And so Arianna left the town, left us to take over La La Land while she opted for New York. We didn't speak for seven years. I think of those times as the dark ages in our family. She tells me sometimes that she envied how close the brothers were. In these moments, I'm grateful for what I had yet I long for what I didn't. I told her when she went away, she became a full person. When all the brothers were with each other so closely for so many years, we kind of didn't really get to develop other aspects of ourselves. We thought our brothers covered all the bases of our humanity, when in reality, we each contain multitudes.

In general, I think families have this secret, unspoken agreement to bind each other to the familiar. Sometimes going away from all that you know gives you space to be what you want.

In my whole family, my little sister Arianna reminds me the most of myself. She looks the most like me of all my siblings, and we're both community builders. Creatively, she not only followed her brothers' path to acting, but she also became a poet like me. I created spaces like DPL— Da Poetry Lounge— the largest weekly open mic venue in Los Angeles and #WeOwn-The8th, an Asian American Arts Collective, while she created her own art collective and magazine, Tard and Feathered. Plus a variety show called Speakeasy, Our Mic the open mic, and currently Palms Up Academy, an arts hub in Historic Filipinotown.

We don't always get along, but I guess when you're that similar, sometimes you don't. I remember once, we hadn't talked in awhile, and I was at my parents' house, where she was staying at the time. And we got to catch up in a very unique way. She read me some new poems, I had my own journal with me— we went back and forth for an hour or two, not discussing the pieces at all, just listening to each other's stories. It gave me such an intimate picture of what we'd each been up to and into, and how she'd been feeling. She's a wonderful, wonderful artist. There are times I know I wasn't there for her, as her big brother, there were times where I should have been there for her more. If she holds that against me, even today, I understand.

Part of this book aims to warn you about the rough patches we hit, as a family and as individuals. I can't warn you away from the unexpected, only from trusting anyone in Hollywood fully. Even after a decade, someone who claims to have your best interests at heart probably does not. I don't mean to be bleak, just practical. We've seen what happens when you let the monster inside the walls. Sometimes in the rise to fame, we are afraid to speak up against the wrongdoings, in fear of losing everything. You can leave memories behind, but the damage will follow you. I'm still so grateful to have my family, to process these blessings and curses together.

13607 1/2

During junior high and high school, I lived in Paramount, CA, a little blue-collar town outside of Los Angeles. When we first went to see the house, my brothers and I didn't want to leave the car. The block was pretty rough. It was the 90's, and we came from living a few years in the suburb of Cerritos, to sitting in the car in a part of the city known as Dogpatch. Also the name of the local gang. The cream and brown one-story house, not unlike a box, was caged in by a metal chain-link fence. It was a far cry from the houses we were used to, and we made a stink about it all. I feel like an asshole now thinking about it. Can you imagine being my dad, trying to buy us a house near LA, and this is what he can afford, and his kids won't even get out of the car? As a kid, I had no idea what it took to buy a house, and can't even begin to think of how my father must have felt, trying to put a roof over his family when his kids didn't even want to get out of the car to look at the place.

Ironically, this house and this neighborhood would forever change my life, and shape who I am today. I think if we'd stayed in middle-class neighborhoods, a whole part of me, that defines me in many ways, would not be in me.

In our little house in Paramount, I lived with my parents, my brothers and sister, plus my mom's brother, Uncle Chet, and her three sisters: my Auntie Nita, my Auntie Bernadette, and Auntie Caroline. Although, my aunts Bernadette and Caroline were just a few years older than me, so they feel closer to cousins than aunts— sisters, even. We all went to high school together. My parents had somewhat of the reputation of getting kids back on the straight and narrow, so other family members would live with us for extended periods of time. At this time we also had my cousin Gibby and our childhood friend Dawny living with us, as well as countless friends that seemed to stay for days, sometimes weeks on end. Minimum, that's 13 people living in this small house at any given moment.

All the girls lived in the house, and all of us boys lived in the separate garage that we affectionately called 13607 ½ , the address of our house. We were teenage artists, exploring whoever we thought we were that week. All of us studied acting and music, and around that time, we obsessed over a film called *Dead Poets Society*. Long before I ever worked beside Robin Williams, that film struck such a chord with us. That little garage became our own Dead Poets Society. We'd write raps and poems, and recite them to each other. Since it was outside the main house, we could sneak in girls. It was still close enough to my parents' bedroom, so we had to be quiet, but this was our place, and adventure ensued. There were no dividing walls in the garage, just 5 to 8 guys living in one space. We had a pool table, a stereo system, two couches that the older guys usually got to sleep in, and the rest of us slept on the floor with a mountain of blankets and pillows.

THE CULT OF ENTERTAINMENT

Family can be a positive or a negative in your life. My entertainment family is an extension of my profession. I'm going to share a story about a situation here that may take your rose-tinted look at Hollywood, and blemish those lenses a bit. But that's how this city works.

Alongside potholes and air pollution, cults are yet another danger in the infrastructure of Hollywood. They sneak up on you. Traps wait in the most unlikely of places. Folks that you think would be smart enough to see what was happening lose themselves to these imaginary worlds.

That being said...I was in a cult.

I studied Scientology for many years. You can read about that group elsewhere. That's not my fight to have today, nor were they even the people to have the biggest impact on me.

My cult was an acting class. Our religion was performance.

It was intense. When I think back on those days, it is very bittersweet. Those were some of the best days of my life. I was filled to the brim with the ideals of a young artist. Studying the greats, and trying out every style with vigor. All the Basco children studied. It began as just Sundays, then spread to three days a week, then five. Scene study and improv and movement and production. For conservatory training, it made sense to sink in that much time. That's not where this goes off the rails. Cults are defined by a number of elements, but one of them is misplaced admiration for a particular person.

For me, that person was Gloria.

When I look back now, it was an abusive relationship. A brilliant teacher, whom I credit for teaching my family how to act. She taught us how to recognize ourselves as artists. Once you come into your creativity like that, what happens is alchemy. Your bones turn to pure gold, and you feel that strength shine within you.

I come from a blue-collar town. I didn't come from artists. But once you're part of that world, your possibilities change. All these forms of beauty— poetry and music and dance and film— are just frivolous forms of entertainment in the regular world. In our world, it is life and death. It's the tool that can change the world. To get there, that's a great thing. That's the cultish thing about the class: once you're there, you feel that you're a part of this blessed and blessing community.

After I left and grew up and healed from that, I read up on cults. You might think it's only the most naive people who get sucked into these schemes, but the defining trait is idealism. If art, for example, is inherently good, then anything you do for the sake of art in the world must be good, right? When you're in this school, you do so much for the betterment of the school and the students, but also to please the leader. When that relationship goes awry for whatever reason...I don't know. It can be abusive.

So then you start losing track of your own career, and what you want in your life in general. You just want to make someone else happy. You can call it a cult, but that can be a business, that can be a production company, a studio. Any person in power with a bunch of idealistic people-pleasers loses track of what the real goals are. You get caught up in trying to placate one person, and all their known or unpredictable wishes. You live in a net of anticipation.

I still have dreams of being back in class and having that same uneasy feeling in my gut. That's when I really understood that I was in an abusive relationship. It affects things in my life now, from romantic relationships to getting involved with new groups. Even the most basic act of trust feels difficult sometimes. But those classes were very important in my life— twenty years of my life that I spent there. I've seen artists become better artists. Even the damage is part of the journey of my life as an artist.

As much as my family and the places I've lived have been part of my journey, one of the biggest influences was this one woman. How could I consider writing this whole book, yet waver between even mentioning her name? It's puzzled me in a lot of ways but I finally realized: as influential as she's been in my life, I look back and, more than anything, I feel ashamed. Like ice melting under my skin.

Gloria was my acting coach.

That alone doesn't sound like anything too shameful. Quite honestly, for many years, it was something I held with honor. See, me and my brothers studied acting with her and in her school for 20 years. Yes, that is not a typo, 20 years. I'm proud of what we learned— we were trained in a way that I don't know if many actors were trained. Yes, we were taught theatrical training, but it went deeper than that: we studied film and television, movement and voice, in a manner that was almost militant.

We started working with her when I was 10, all of us.

I often wonder about my parents, who they were in those days. Who would leave everything they knew in their lives, all of their family and friends— who would leave all that to support the dreams of their kids?

I was only 10 years old, Dion was 8 turning 9— I mean, it was a big risk. As the story goes, or at least how my mom would tell it: we came to town as breakdancers and quickly discovered that LA isn't about dancers. It's Hollywood, it's about the movies and television and that's about actors. We were about to become actors. But since our experience had only been as dancers, my mom knew that we needed training. She went the the Samuel French bookstore on Sunset, that bookstore with all the plays and books on the industry, listings for agents and casting directors and, yes, for acting schools. My mother took that book and she prayed. She said, *My kids must become actors, and they must learn how to act. Please, can you lead me to the right place?*

My mother opened the book and she circled a name, and that name was Gloria.

What is so crazy about this woman? Why were we so afraid of her? How did she cut so deep that I still have nightmares of being back in class, shaking with dread? Why don't I feel in control of my life, the way she controlled me for years?

I can feel it in my relations with my family, my brothers, with women in my life. She shaped me from such a young age.

I'll try to write about it, and see if I can uncover something that can give me some relief. I hate to think I'll look back at what I've written, and feel that it's inconsequential, or not as big of a deal as it is in my head.

I can tell you this, that class fostered an emotionally abusive relationship. People called it a cult. I used to shrug that stuff off, explaining that others didn't understand, but as I look back, I see it really was a cult. She took us from breakdancing kids to well-trained actors, but it all had a price.

We studied at her conservatory — we actually help build up this conservatory, from an afternoon class on Sunday to a full schedule of classes: speech, film, and, of course, scene study. She taught the scene study classes and hired others, including my brother Derek, to teach the beginning class.

She was a great teacher, and I still look back fondly on all the work we produced at that time in my life. I produced some twenty-eight or so showcases, as well as being in all of them— even if I was shooting another project at the time, I'd race to the theatre to hit the stage, then race back to set. Maybe that fondness, the blend of fear and love in that class, makes it so hard to move on.

Gloria got us to believe that we were artists. We watched all the classic films and read all the plays, between acting out scenes from the great works of Tennessee Williams, David Mamet, Shakespeare, Arthur Miller, and Clifford Odets. Not a bad bookshelf to start off with.

With modern films, we discussed them not as fans, but as peers that would be creating these works someday. She changed my life, she really did. She impacted all of my brothers and close friends that studied with her— many of us still close today. Yet, she fucked us up too. Even if I'm grateful for how Gloria shaped my skills as an actor, there's so much more to my life than performance. Parts of me that she had no right to control.

She'd tell us that there is good control and bad control, but it was dominance no matter how she cloaked it. It hurts to know that I never stood up to her, not until the day we walked out, though there were many times before when I wanted to. She'd been in my life since I was ten years old. I couldn't help but idealize her as some maternal figure, who knew so much about the world I so badly wanted to join.

With this intense theatrical training, you talk about emotions all day long. How your character feels, how you feel, and what memories you can pull from yourself to bridge that gap. And I was a child, discovering who I was as a person while trying to carve a path in a new city. There were so many opportunities for emotional manipulation that I can only see now, as an adult with experience in the industry.

Gloria had a way of getting too involved, inviting herself into my private life. I want to believe she wasn't conscious of what she did to her students. She dictated who they should date, whether or not they should have a relationship with their parents.

Several times she made me break up with women— I don't know why I let her do that to me. It went so far once that she made me break up with a girl over email, then BCC Gloria to prove I had done it. Her reasoning: I truly don't know. She feared I wasted my time on women. Even if I did, it would never have been her call.

What woke me up is when she made me break up with a girl I was truly in love with. We shot a film together and fell in love on set. I hid the relationship from Gloria, and when she found out she lost her mind, calling me from LA to Toronto, shouting at me over the phone. I continued the relationship in secret while on location, and when I got back to LA, it got to a point where I was forced to break up with her.

I'm really ashamed of myself for that one. Love is supposed to be what you swim oceans for, and I let this woman crush a relationship I truly loved, and wanted. When it happened, I was devastated. I was still in the group for maybe a year, but I was a shadow of myself, just going through the motions.

Throughout your whole life, you carry whatever was put upon you as a young person. As new students, Gloria assigned us classical actors to study as distant mentors. Over some 20 years later, these actors still resonate with me and my brothers. I remember Dion was Clark Gable: carefree, brash, a drinker. Darion was the Brando guy—deep thinker, passionate, sexy. Me, I had Montgomery Clift. I read his biographies, watched all of his movies and loved them like a new language. My favorite film of all time is still *A Place in the Sun*, and, all these years later, I still like to think of myself in a Monty Clift sort of way. I wonder about getting heroes assigned to us when we were so young, that were not models we picked ourselves. As I think back now, I realize all those actors were dead before we were even born. More than anything else, Gloria gave us ghosts.

I sometimes fear that I'm stuck in my youth.

I know, Peter Pan Syndrome and all. Stop laughing.

I get that it's the thesis here. I write often enough that I know my own patterns. I'm not unaware of the situation. There's a lot of evidence.

In this town, that mindset must be bleeding into the drinking water, because everyone here suffers from it. My whole world seems centered around adolescence, and that's complicated. Few people have ever been in this place in the way I've been in this place.

I still play teenagers today in animated projects, and it seems I have a never-ending fanbase of teenagers that find my work resonates with them decades later. I admit, now in my forties, when I think of myself or envision myself, I don't really see myself in a very "manly" way—I feel like a boy, still. There are certain things in life I haven't done yet that I consider marks of manhood, like getting married and having children. If I saw myself on-screen and didn't know how old I was, I couldn't guess my age. Maybe late 20s? It might sound pathetic, and perhaps it is. As a child actor, sometimes I feel stuck in this pretend world, this Never Neverland where I play dress-up, and the rest of the world's rules escape me.

HOOK

Before I even considered myself an actor, I worked in the industry. I was one of the lucky kids that walked into their first audition and wound up getting hired. Casting knew this was my first audition, and, recognizing I had something, gave me a smaller co-starring role. Fewer lines, but regardless, I'd just booked my first job. Now, I didn't get any of that other information until years later, when the kid they did hire told me in our 20s. That kid, Kenny Morrison, had become a friend and had a good career too, playing Atreyu in *The Neverending Story* sequel. Funny thing is, this role that I got hired for was playing Native American— and no, I'm not Native, and neither is Kenny. We're both Filipino, and we were playing Indigenous Americans on a reservation for a television show called *The Wizard* starring David Rappaport, who I knew from the movie *Time Bandits*. I don't remember much about the episode, except that we had to be there early, and it was dusty. I had a few lines, and I remember going to school on set for the first time. Legally, when you're a child actor, you have to attend class for 3 hours per work day and complete work assigned by your normal school. I spent many hours in studio school— learning some things, mostly talking with my studio teachers. I finished high school, but I never went on to college. My education would unfold in a different way.

After *The Wizard*, I began booking work pretty steadily. Through studying, auditioning, and booking jobs, I grew into a working actor at a very young age. My family was still modest, with my father as the main breadwinner, a telephone man working for Pac Bell in the Bay Area and then AT&T when we moved to LA.

My mom raised us five kids, and guided our acting careers. When you're a child actor, your whole life depends on the willingness and support of your parents. Not only do they need to drive you to endless auditions, but they also have to be with you on set— you need a legal guardian until the age of 16. If my mom wasn't there for all this, I wouldn't have a career today. Many thankless (sorry to say) car rides, hours on sound stages. But we kept driving, and I kept working.

I've mentioned before that I don't really like the spotlight. So finding myself on TV as a kid created some complicated situations. Being a small town breakdancer from a small town and becoming successful was so heady — when you win a breakdancing competition in your hometown, everyone is hyped about it. My brothers and I were hometown stars. I just remember being very young, and these older guys thinking I was cool. I had this sense of wonder at what the world could bring me if I worked at my craft. So when my brothers and I got into acting, it was just another step. Being an artist comes with this feeling like you're special. It's not even believing that you're special, it's the feeling of people looking at you like you're special.

So as a kid, it's like, *are* you special? Are you not special? You really start to feel that awe and wonderment when you go to public school and people see you on TV. You wrestle with that.

Then you leave your hometown for LA and the scale is... universal. You want to be excited about everything you do, but you might not be proud of everything you do. You want to play cool characters, but you could be cast in something that kids wouldn't touch with a longboard. This was part of the anxiety of being on TV and also going to public school. Like, you might see me across the class in algebra, and then again on-screen when you get home.

I remember doing a CBS Afterschool Special, a TV movie called *15 and Getting Straight*. I was 13, and the project co-starred Drew Barrymore and Corey Feldman. They were actual movie stars. The first day I met Drew, I was in awe. She was a few months older and two, three planets away from me. And Corey could command his own galaxy. I knew they both were coming off their own bouts with drugs and alcohol, so this project must have hit close to home for them.

I played a Mexican kid, dealing drugs within the rehab. It was just a small group of us teenage actors, but I was the youngest, trying to keep up. It definitely felt like hanging with the cool kids. Doing scenes on set and rehearsing was always fun, but since we were kids, we also went to studio school, so we spent most of the day together. I do remember once when we broke for lunch— Corey being Corey, he wasn't really trying to have what they were serving. We were teenagers, he wanted Taco Bell, so we rolled out! We piled into his car, a black convertible shining like a new sun. Squished in with the cast, it was the first time I ever rode in a BMW. Music blaring with something Corey wrote as he drove just a little too fast.

There was a whole thing about us and the special in TV Guide. That was the true sign you made it. Back then, my family would gather around the TV and watch it together. It was slightly embarrassing to a degree, because honestly? I'm the middle child. I don't really care to be the center of attention. I don't like my own birthday parties. I like being social, but I don't necessarily want everybody looking at me.

Yet for all my fidgeting in the living room, starting out my life in this business felt good. Like I belonged. It was light years different from the world I grew up in, but I wanted to belong like nothing else. So often in this town, you don't know if you're part of the picture or just outside the frame. You fight to catch up, or build a completely different universe of your own.

I'm proud that I got to act alongside some of the biggest names of my generation. I did *The Wonder Years* with Fred Savage and a movie after that. I'm working on an animated project with Danica Mckeller right now, even. I worked with Will Smith on *The Fresh Prince of Bel-Air,* and did shows like *Highway To Heaven* with Michael Landon, who I grew up watching in Bonanza reruns every day, after *The Price Is Right.* One of my fondest memories is when Robin Givens leaned over to me during a table read and whispered, "Don't you hate being the new kid on set?" I just stared back and nodded. Sometimes it feels like you're the only person on Earth who gets anxious. Those shared moments are so precious— they remind you that you're never alone.

And I felt isolated pretty often back then. I was working so much as a kid actor, it made me uncomfortable. In high school, I had a pager that my mom would buzz if I had an audition. Her code was 303: put it sideways, and it reads "MOM". It means "I'm coming to pick you up after school, be ready to audition."

So my friends went to the library after school, to study, to hang out with girls or get doughnuts — and I couldn't do any of that stuff. I had to go sit in traffic for an hour, and run lines with my mom. I can hear you rolling your eyes at me. Of course you think it would be cool to have a little machine that could ding and get you out of school. But I knew that I was missing out on friendship, and exchanging that for actual work. The glamour and excitement wore off quick for me. It became my normal.

I'd have fights with my mom, that I just wanted to be normal. But we didn't move the whole family to Hollywood to be normal. I even stood up girls at school dances when I was younger because I couldn't get off the set. I'd want to go on a field trip with the rest of my class and, during an audition, I asked when the project would shoot. It was always exactly when the trip would have been. To this day, the business interrupts my life. I'm still missing weddings, holidays, anything beyond my work calendar. The normalcy of that kind of life is forever secondary to what comes up in my career. I have no steady work schedule.

If I'd lived closer to the city, at least there would've been other actor kids to hang out with. Commiserate with. At least to know them, as peers. I was a little too far away for that.

I consider what might've been different about this childhood, and the man I've become, if I'd had social media back then. I'm not complaining about *kids today*. I just wonder if my outlook on the world, and on myself, would be different if I'd come up taking selfies. If I could transport myself elsewhere at the touch of a button, whether that be downtown LA or a virtual world. Or if I could curate my days, make everything around me look better than it actually was. How would that have shaped my reaction to the house I grew up in?

Being a kid is tough, and even tougher is finding a balance when you have such little control over your life. That's why it was hard to even pause and consider What Could Be when I got an audition for this new upcoming film, *Hook*.

I've seen one-hit wonder bands with a certain sense of humor joke: "Hey, we're about to do the song you came to hear. Get your phones out now. We'll wait." I'm not a one-hit wonder.

That said, get your phones out now. I know what you came here to see.

At the time, my little brother Dion got an audition for another role in *Hook*. We all had different agents and managers; I called my manager up like, "My little brother's auditioning for the Peter Pan movie with Robin Williams, can you get me anything?"

People are often surprised to hear that everyone in our family had different agents and managers. That's just the smartest way to do it. No conflicts of interest. It also meant that our parents had to trust that teams of strangers had our best interests at heart. This may not come as a shock, but that would not always be the case.

I got the audition for Rufio, but not just me: my other brother Darion got an audition for the same role. That's the dynamic — it's hard to be an actor in Hollywood. Even harder to be an actor of color, an Asian actor, a Filipino American. Even harder to be one of the Basco brothers, all around the same age. To regularly audition against each other for every single role. To win, other people I love had to lose.

This made for uncomfortable drives home.

We learned to deal, and grow with it. Every actor must realize in their own way that when you're hired, you get the job because of you, regardless of the role. If they want Dante, they can't hire Dion. You can't take it personally. Whoever got the job was putting food on the table, as well. But we were kids. So we didn't think that way. We wanted to win. We came up through breakdance, so we know how to compete through art. Through battles. That's what every audition is. You go in to win, and it hurts to lose. I've lost things that I wanted, that they got.

Me and Darion both got the audition, and we each saw the other perform, and what they brought to the character. Neither of us was better or worse, just his take on it and my take on it. That's how acting works— it's just playing the character to your ability.

The film was about Peter Pan and the Lost Boys, but a version of them that hadn't existed before. I had no clue what this character was supposed to be. I didn't even know who he was. I just thought that he was a bad boy, which was fine. We're brown. If you're brown in Hollywood, you play the bad guy. A large percentage of the roles I've played were that.

We went through the dialogue, and there was a confrontation scene with Peter Pan. So we went over it with our acting coach, and dressed ourselves up in what we thought Lost Boys would wear. There must be a picture somewhere. I had a printed, oversized shirt tied up with leaves and leather wristbands. You try these little things that might distinguish you from the lineup. Darion and I went together to the taped audition, and met the casting director. It felt good. We thanked our acting coach for rehearsing it with us. I got a call back two days later, saying "Steven Spielberg would like to meet you." My brother didn't get the call back. We were close— so close that people thought we were twins growing up. I was sad that he didn't get to go forward with it.

It was a Universal film, so we went to Universal Studios, in the backlot. We got to go back there, me and my mom, in her van. Not a minivan, a big van. There's a section in the back that looks like a Spanish villa: those are Steven Spielberg's offices, and Amblin Entertainment. Back in the day, the rumor was that Steven Spielberg had an arcade in his offices. This was pre-Playstation, so we spent hours in the mall arcade as kids. They opened the door, and right by the secretary's office, there were enough video games to entertain half of LAUSD. I played for what felt like a whole summer before someone tapped me on the shoulder. Spielberg was ready to see me. They escorted me into his office, and there the legend stood, bright as a movie poster in his Hawaiian shirt.

We sat down and started talking while he looked at my picture and resume. Steven asked about my other roles. At that point, I'd done a karate film with Paramount called *The Perfect Weapon*. We talked about the street kid I played in that movie, on the run from the Chinese mafia. I told him what it was like playing a street urchin, and compared it to Rasto Rizzo. He was like, "What?" I said, "Yeah, Rasto Rizzo, from *Midnight Cowboy*." Then we were talking about Dustin Hoffman, who was actually playing Captain Hook himself. So here was a fifteen-year-old kid chatting away to Steven Spielberg about *Midnight Cowboy*, and he was just looking at me. Somewhere in the middle of the conversation, I asked him if he wanted to do a read, and he was like, "Nah, you don't gotta read it." I was like, "What?"

He replied, "You don't have to read it, I just wanted to meet you." We talked a bit longer, and I left let down because I didn't read the lines for him. I went back to my mom, who asked about the meeting. I was so sure I lost it. I explained that we just didn't even read the script, just talked. I swore I was out.

As we left Universal Studios, we crashed into the intercom. Yeah. We crashed into the intercom and rolled on. What are you gonna do? It didn't look promising. But also, I had five years of Hollywood experience. You win some, you lose some.

A few days later, they offered me the job.

I got a call from my manager in the middle of acting class, and my coach made us celebrate. But you can get fired at any moment, so I try to stay even-keeled. Later on, during shooting, I was sitting in full costume, on a barrel by the pirate ship. I asked Steven, "Hey, how did you hire me? When I met you, I never really auditioned for you. I've never booked a job like that." He said, "Dante, out of all the kids we auditioned for your role, when I saw your tape...you were the only kid that scared me." That was the end of the conversation. That's how I got *Hook*.

People outside of Hollywood don't know that that's how these things can work. Auditions can just be a test that you're Cool To Work With. That process can be more nerve-racking than a script-based audition, I assure you. When you're a more established actor, no one questions your abilities. Even now as I'm producing or directing a film and I'm interviewing actors, it's more about "Who are you?" Let me sit and see if we gel. It's less about your ability to do the role. Your past work tells me that you can do the role. But as a child actor, you don't go through that.

Things moved quickly. We didn't start shooting until January, but I was sword fighting and rehearsing months earlier.

I loved sword fighting. One of my proudest achievements in that film is my absolute lack of a stunt double. All the sword fighting you see is me. I think that's also part of what makes Rufio so authentic, the honesty in his character that draws people close. Stage combat is more of a dance than a martial art, or real fight. You might have experience in both those fields, but you're a dancer. You're learning choreography. Sword fighting outside of the stage is still footwork and battle dancing, but with swords. It's about understanding that language: parries and foot movement, and reacting in real time. You go to the studio in Culver City, full of literal Olympic fencers. As a kid, there was nothing cooler than taking up a sword and learning how to use it. Star Wars. Errol Flynn. Robin Hood. Excalibur and King Arthur. The clash of steel on steel beat through all of our dreams.

A fencing instructor built my skills in sword fighting. To this day, I feel like I could fight with a sword. We also had stage combat instructors teaching us techniques for stage fighting. I went a few days a week to the city, just to get those movements in my bones. They'd take me out of school for sword fighting. It was a blast.

I remember the first time I met Robin Williams was at a sword training session. Robin came in unshaven; his beard was so thick. We learned sword fighting together, and it was pretty amazing to begin our relationship with that.

I don't remember the first exchanges; I was always a little standoff-ish with big stars. There was a bit of reverence. I never want to be up anybody's ass. Especially Robin Williams.

I didn't know who Dustin Hoffman was until I studied film, but Robin was always part of our household, from *Mork and Mindy* to *Happy Days*. Then *Dead Poets Society* spun into my teenage life as one of my favorite films, and it holds that spot to this day. That's who Robin Williams was to me, a teacher before we ever met. I shared that with him, and he became a true mentor. There's a picture of us together, with him wearing a hat that I'd made at the Compton Swap Meet, "O Captain, my Captain" emblazoned on the front.

At first, it was just me practicing with the sword fighting guy, then Robin came along. The other kids didn't join us until later, when we came to the Sony lot. That was a month or two prior to filming, but because I had a different role, I had private lessons. Kids of all ages were in the Lost Boys. As I look back, twelve and fifteen felt like different worlds, as if I was basically an adult as opposed to these tweens. After you turn thirty, it feels like everyone's the same age.

There were different sections of Lost Boys, younger and older. I had my crew of older skateboarder guys. The younger kids were doing their own thing, and I was the adversarial type, even to them. I was the mean leader. When you're on set as a kid, you're not treated like a kid. They're paying you adult money. Most of the time, you're the only kid on the set. I was mostly hanging out with adult actors and crew all day. Even though I was a kid, everyone assumed I'd act like an adult.

It was a weird dichotomy to live in the garage of a house with eighteen people, and then go to my trailer on the Sony lot with people preparing food for me like a Hollywood star. It was something you get used to though—it really is part of the job. People wait on you, to a degree. Some people abuse it; I never wanted to. It could be a pitfall for a kid that didn't have the sort of foundational boundaries that my family instilled in me. Growing up, I was equally happy talking about poetry in a garage as I was to act with Robin Williams.

Hook started shooting in January of 1991. The Lost Boys shot earlier in the process; I didn't start acting until later than everybody else. They were still putting my look together. Rufio is iconic, right? People dress up as him. Back then, he was a new character. The Lost Boys, when you look at them, are dressed to reflect different time eras. Some of them dress like Newsies, others from the '50s. These great artists were doing sketches of my character's look, because they didn't know what it was going to be.

Then the amazing wardrobe people get a hold of me. I've played a lot of street kids, and when wardrobe people try to dress you tough, it's usually some middle-class white woman's idea of tough, and it's...not. It's not cool. But it's a fantasy-land, right? The first thing they gave me was red tights. Which felt like more of a red flag. Then I had to put hole-y jeans over it. You've got to realize, we were in the early '90s. My daily wear was baggy everything, and now they were putting me in skin-tight jeans with red tights underneath? There was also a skin-tight shirt cut off at the midriff. My belly button was showing. I had my belly button showing. Then, they wanted me to put on this leather jacket with fringe all over it. I had on red boots and a leather loincloth with fringe. It felt like a goth cowboy, but I couldn't say anything because they're all artists. You've gotta let people do their art. Once I was done, I was like, "Maybe it's not going to be the actual outfit. There were tons of drawings, right?" Then they brought in the hair and makcup. They played with my hair by blowing it out big, and they went, "What about a mohawk? What about *three* mohawks?" A tri-hawk.

This was an all-day event. They were designing as they dressed me. Now I've got this punk rock country-western...what am I? My hair felt so big. They brought me on set, and all the Lost Boys were doing a scene and Steven was directing them.

He turned around, and he looked at me and said, "Hm. Yes. YES."

I was like, "Yeah? Yeah? Oh, NO!"

So I was stuck with the look. This was the character. This was what I was working with. But the designers must have known something that I didn't, because almost three decades later, it's iconic. I get Instagram pictures every day of people dressed up like him, whole clothing lines inspired by that look. The amount of songs that allude to Rufio—rappers like Drake and Flo Rida shout out Rufio. Skrillex has a song called "Banga-rang." He's part of people's dialogue.

But back in time, back on set, the Lost Boys had a strange way of working. They kept switching their lines, and it became a competition over which Boy could say the lines better. I had different lines, so I didn't have to be in that same space. Certain kids started to stand out, and Dustin Hoffamn would be there on the set, creating a rapport with them. He ultimately became a huge mentor to me on set and in my life, but these first few weeks were hard.

He would be in my ear, saying subversive things to me. He wasn't in costume, but he was very Captain Hook-y. Jimmy Madio is one of my lifelong friends, and was one of the Lost Boys. Dustin would mutter, "Oh, Jimmy's part is getting bigger." This would make me doubt myself.

This is before I'm even acting.

He was freaking me out.

So I'd go home and freak out.

Thankfully, I could vent to my acting coach about what happened on set. She was keen on Dustin Hoffman and his career. She explained to me that he's a method actor. *The* method actor, actually. He had a reputation in town as an actor and as a person. She said that I had to create a relationship with him, as Captain Hook himself.

"You are a power on that set, within the confines of the film. You're another, younger Peter Pan, an adversary to Captain Hook. He wants to overpower you." I was like, "I don't want to be an adversary, I want him to like me! He's fucking Dustin Hoffman! This is not real life! Why is he a jerk?!" This is the thing about sets: there are so many dynamics happening within that ecosystem. It's like you're back in high school again.

It's complicated to look back at Dustin Hoffman and how he treated me. It was scary. He was playing games with me the way he played games with actors he trusted. At the time, I was feeling super stressed out. There were rumors that Dustin could be hard on his fellow actors, and he can be. My acting coach helped me devise a plan to deal with him: let him know who you are. Respect and know who he is. So I did.

I would come to the set to watch him work. It wasn't manipulative— I wanted to see that greatness at work. I explain to young artists that when I was fifteen, I got to work with gods in the industry. So if any of us are in the presence of greatness, we have the responsibility to be in the moment and soak that in. To be the most attentive, most active listener of all. Watching Spielberg direct. Watching Hoffman act. It was like hearing Mozart conduct a symphony. I was just old enough and artistic enough to do that. I'd be on set reading his biographies. I'd watch his movies. I went up to him and asked about a scene in *Lenny*, "What were you thinking during that?" "I just watched *Kramer vs. Kramer* again last night, I love that scene. What's the process? How did that work out?"

Tennis players play the game to their competition. Actors know actors. Acting is not just you acting alone, it's a conversation with the world around you. So when an actor encounters another actor, you can feel it.

When I started trying to connect with Dustin as an actor, our relationship changed. It became less adversarial. He's always had an edge, but he became a mentor. When I was about to film my death scene, I knocked on his door and told him that I'd never done a death scene, and asked for advice.

"What day is it?" he asked.

"It's on Wednesday," I said.

"I'll be there," he replied.

He became my acting coach for the day and walked me through the death scene. To work with a legend, and be validated by him, really put me through the emotions. Invaluable. I wish I could remember all the advice he offered at the time. Climbing fully into the scene, understanding when to do it heavy, things like that. Trying to find the truth in the moment.

Feel it. He let me know, "You've got the stuff, kid. Trust what you're doing."

The first time I saw *Hook*, like most actors in any project, was the premiere. It was an interesting premiere because it was such a big movie, that it premiered in several different theaters in LA at the same time. I think there were three different screenings, with a few charities involved. It was a unique film for its time. I remember I saw it in Century City, at a theater that no longer exists. But these memories play on.

I'd had other movies, but there was no big premiere that came out like that. It was my first red carpet ever. I remember taking a lot of pictures, but I don't know that it made a heavy impression on me. Red carpets are cool and uncomfortable at the same time. I get it. You come to get to know a lot of the photographers because some of them also do paparazzi stuff. They're usually polite enough if you just say what's up. I saw Don Johnson and Melanie Griffith with their kids walking down too. I worked with both of them after that. Don and I worked on Nash Bridges together in San Francisco, and I did a movie with Antonio Banderas called *Take The Lead*, when he was married to Melanie Griffith. We talked about meeting on the red carpet of Hook, it was crazy. Hollywood is weird like that.

The drama of the premiere, to me, had nothing to do with flashing lights. My family almost didn't make it to the premiere. On the way, we got into a big fight in the family van. At that time it was about my hair, I don't know. Me and my mom were arguing with the whole family there. She didn't want to go to the premiere anymore. It was wild to have my calm, careful mother suddenly become a fighter the night of my first big premiere.

My hair was too high for her liking. It was the 90's, and we all wore crazy hairdos. She didn't like it. In life, there's always the apparent event and the actual event. The apparent event was the hair. What was actually going on? We were all so close to the edge then. We almost didn't even leave the house, just sat in the driveway. My brother filmed the whole fight on the family camcorder. I've never seen the video, but it's out there in my mom's attic.

There's so much that went on, within my sister's life at the time, and me leaving my old agent and manager. At the highest height of your career, some of the lowest, most awful things could happen. As a kid back then, I felt they were connected, that I caused anything bad that happened to my family with my success. I feel I still carry that guilt, no matter how much I've grown.

So my memory of that premiere is that mostly of the fight. We almost didn't get to the show. It was a very tumultuous time in life. I was fifteen, trying to become a man. When you're young, and you don't know what to do, you feel powerless.

But we made it. The Bascos always make it in the end.

The red carpet and the movie went by in a blur, to be honest. The cast was split between different events, with Dustin Hoffman and I at one theater and Robin at another. Everyone met back up at Sony studios for a wild wrap party. They had it at one of the soundstages, with the pirate ship from the movie as the centerpiece. I met all kinds of people that night, some that would become friends for a long time.

I remember meeting Punky Brewster that night, Soleil Moon Frye, and hanging out with her for years to come. I met another Filipino actor that night, Ernie Reyes, Jr. I'm always regarded as the first Filipino American actor, but Ernie came before me. He was in the show *Sidekick*, and *The Last Dragon* movie. He always looked out for me at clubs, and to this day I have a lot of love for him.

The young Hollywood scene back then was fun, but it had more than its share of danger and drama too. I didn't feel peer pressure as seriously because I had my brothers everywhere, even at parties. We were all just kids growing up on studio lots. We wanted to meet cool people we knew from the movies we watched like anyone else, but we actually had that chance, dozens of times over. We wanted to maybe get a drink, dance, and kiss someone cute. We were what you would be if you were in Hollywood. You could rebel against parents and tradition, but you might wind up doing that in a nightclub near teenage Leonardo DiCaprio. What bothered was how some of these kids saw "thug life" as a trend. I was living in the hood, and all that wild shit went down around me. I'm not pretending. That was my environment. A gun got pulled on my brother when he walked home from middle school. Watching some actor trash a hotel room was funny because it was like, look at this tourist in the world of violence. That was my only bit of judgement. Like, these dudes were really trying it. I came to party and get away from the bullshit, and they wanted to manufacture bullshit?! Okay. Can we just get to the cute girls?

Still, it was a different time when Young Hollywood meant some beers and bad jokes. But it's not recorded online, so it doesn't chase you for the rest of your life. There was a certain innocence to it. Hollywood works like a graduating class. You go back to your ten-year reunion, and see the kids you grew up with. Or you don't. The town devours them. People leave the business. People make mistakes, people die. For a lot of them, I still want to know what kind of person they ended up becoming. Not what we see online, but who they are in private these days. You have to hope there's room for folks to change.

Anyway, that wrap party was special, and I remember one of the craziest moments was when I talked to a mermaid from the movie. She was saying that one of the mermaids got to kiss Robin Williams, and she didn't get to kiss anybody. I told her that Robin got to kiss all the mermaids, and I didn't get to kiss anyone. Then she looked right at me and kissed me, and I was like, "Oh, shit!"

I was fifteen or sixteen when it premiered. I lost my virginity during *Hook*, also. I'm talking about all that teenage stuff that goes on coupled with family drama and tragedy, but everything was heightened because of *Hook*. It really shaped me.

That first screening flew by. I can't remember the film itself. But I had other opportunities. When big studio films come out, you go to the premiere and you end up seeing it at different screenings. I probably saw it two or three other times in the neighborhood with family. You watch and try to enjoy it with the rest of the audience. I thought it was fun as a kid, the magic of it all. But also, I personally don't love watching myself on screen. Doing the projects is why I do it. To watch it later on isn't the same experience as acting. As an actor, you're an ingredient in the meal. After those first few times, I didn't watch the movie for years. Decades, maybe. There are some things I've done that I still haven't seen.

For a lot of actors, it's uncomfortable to watch yourself. We shoot videos or film all the time. We're not watching any of these damn videos. It's way more fun to watch other people's recordings for inspiration. With your own, you're too close. You see your faults and you're looking at stuff that no one else could notice.

But *Hook*, I've seen enough now to have thoughts. I appreciate the film as an adult now, who can understand Peter Pan in a different light. He's an adventurer before he becomes a symbol of static youth, you know? And seeing myself as a teenager, preserved in such an intimate and fantastical way, is its own journey. Under the costume, I remember so much of who I was as a real person then. My insecurities, my hopes. As a kid watching it, I waited on the edge of the velvet theater seat for the film to take us to Neverland. Even though if I'd seen those sets getting built, and knew every plank and water blast, the magic of film transformed them to a new dream.

I still loved the practice of filmmaking. I grew up with my teacher telling me about Maggie Smith, and I was so awed by her on set. Phil Collins worked for a day or two on set, too. He was one of the biggest pop stars in the world in those days, and I was such a big fan. There were moments like that that excited me, but it was tied up with the trauma that my family had to process. It was like we were walking through a cloud.

There's a lot of this that I'm working out here on the page. If the Bascos had been one of those Old Hollywood families, we could have had our enemies destroyed. We were in a much different situation. We were a green family, just rolling along. So much went on with the management company, from shady business to real evil. By the same token, there was also all of this success going on for me. I didn't know who to turn to. I was a fifteen year old kid that should have been able to feel like he was on top of the world. I should have been able to enjoy this.

But in the movie, Rufio gets killed. That's the moral, old as stone: innocence cannot survive. This is the town, and that's part of how the town works. When you play here, the greatest things can and will happen, and the worst things, consequently, can and will happen too. That's part of it.

We didn't know Rufio would die until a week before we shot the scene. There were all these alternate endings. One we never shot, but tested, has the Lost Boys coming back to the real world with Peter Pan at the end. They get back to the window, and Peter Banning takes us in. If you watch the movie, there's no lead-up to me dying, it's very abrupt. For years, the fans from that generation talk about the death of Rufio. I read a blog post some time ago about how the first traumatic moment in that blogger's life was the death of Rufio.

And he doesn't just die. He gets impaled by a sword. It *is* traumatic.

There were actually talks of us doing a Lost Boys series, but the contract never got signed. Then when I got killed, I worried that my character died because I didn't sign the contract. But when I talked to the writer of *Hook*, he said no. He explained that Rufio was always going to die. Peter Pan gets his kids out of Neverland because of the actual danger they faced. With Rufio dead, Peter's stakes rise. We kill pirates. Pirates kill Lost Boys. The Neverland story is a fairytale, in the old sense. So that's what my character represented beyond a Disney cartoon. I think that's one of the reasons why people feel so attached to Rufio: the death is a shock. It's a James Dean thing, to a degree. It's very unnatural for it to happen so abruptly, to a kid that redeems himself.

Our movie is an adaptation of an incredibly racist animation, adapted itself from an incredibly racist book, but I didn't grasp that aspect of it as a kid. One of the Lost Boys was Native American. I did a comic convention in North Dakota, and that was the first time I was around a large Native American community. There were so many Native American kids and adults in the audience. When I met them afterwards, they explained the importance of Rufio to them. They connected with Rufio as Native American to a degree. Which, I guess, builds upon my entire career to that point playing races and ethnicities that I certainly was not.

As a person of color in America, to give voice to any community is important. With representation, I want to be very keen on what we're doing there, especially in the era that we're in now. You try to help tell a story, but in the end, the audience is part of that process. You can't predict that reaction most times, they will receive the story collectively and individually.

Hook occupies this impossibly large chunk of my life. Knowing that, I'm just lucky that it aged so well. It's a throwback to another time of filmmaking. A practical tactility. Like how *Star Wars* used to be. CGI stuff is getting more sophisticated every year, more realistic. When you see the old-school practical effects like pirate ships, it holds up in a different way. When I look at the film now, it still speaks to keeping the kid alive in you.

The whole wonderment of Neverland remains in that film. That's magic. The invisible food coming to life, that imagination is still there. Dustin Hoffman's performance is still larger than life, it's all there. It's just ironic to me now as an adult, to realize that I'm part of this fairytale. Somehow, this Filipino brown kid is part of a fairytale. A living, breathing thing. People dress up like Hook and Pan and Tinkerbell, and Rufio too.

I'm in my forties now, and my first big breakthrough role was playing this Lost Boy. But now that Lost Boy is captured on celluloid and at any point, I can go back and watch myself at fifteen. Literally trapped in time as a kid. I don't feel much melancholy about it; it's a beautiful part of Hollywood history as well as my own. I feel so lucky that it's become a cult classic, too. All of us on Neverland flash in the background of other people's childhoods. Holding that space in the collective memory is an honor.

People will ask if I ever regret playing Rufio. This thing that shaped my life but also made me "Rufio" to people that have run into me on the street for decades. It limited me in some ways. It lifted me up in some ways. It has always been an elaborate set of emotions to unpack.

Being Rufio, and being Rufio forever now — I think it was something I struggled with when I was younger. Now that I'm further away from it, it's more ironic than anything. As a young actor, you're just trying to get your next job. I was so impacted by one character, and it was hard to move on from that. Rufio was confident, funny, flawed. A full character. They just weren't writing roles for people of color that often, roles beyond a caricature. And trying to shake that for many years was kind of hard. But now, he's just a cool piece of my resume. People come to Hollywood to do something memorable. Most people will never get that chance. Even people that work all the time, it's rare to find a character that could mean so much.

I feel very fortunate to have one of those guys on my resume. In my life now, I've been Rufio longer than I haven't been Rufio, so at any given time, it comes up in public. Somewhere, I'll get it. Someone will shout it out to me, always in good energy and good vibes. It means something positive to a lot of people, and it's always brought goodwill to me. I'm so proud of what I brought to that character. Rufio served as a milestone for the representation of the Asian community at large. We can look back and appreciate him as part of the lineage in America, from *Joy Luck Club* to *Crazy Rich Asians*.

It is impossible for me to talk about who I've become without thinking of Robin Williams. Like the rest of us in the production, I was lucky to work with him as an actor, and witness firsthand the magic of what made him a legend—the wit and otherworldly improvisational skills— as well as see him lift the morale of an entire movie set onto his shoulders. He kept everyone laughing as they worked long hours for months on end. And at the same time, I was fortunate to spend so many mornings in the makeup chair just talking with him about poetry. Soft-spoken and introspective under the noise of hair dryers, he discussed Walt Whitman and Charles Bukowski with me like we were true peers. Like millions of others, I was always delightfully surprised by the performances Robin crafted with such care and genius. With his passing, I can't help but feel, along with my generation, the loss of my childhood. We lost him as a culture with his wondrous work on-screen, but I also feel it so personally in my memories of him.

I suppose we can't stay in Neverland forever.

POST-HOOK

My career continued.

I've always had work. To me, the labor looks the same. In every project, I come to the table and I invest all that I have in it. I do my process. I learn my role. I find my space with the other actors. I show up to set, and I make sure I give the best performance that I can. Then I move on. That's the end of my work, and that's when editors and directors and marketing people take over. I have no control over that final product, but that was never my job. There's great value in recognizing the elements you can and cannot control.

One of those elements I cannot control is what my work looks like to the outside world. Er. Let me be more specific: I cannot control what status the world applies to my work.

Pop culture as a whole carries with it an unnatural set of metrics, some good and many arbitrary. How do you measure a piece of art? This issue arises with some frequency, and we're always, as a culture, attempting to apply new systems to it. There's a box office number that you can place on the amount of money a film brings in. There a Rotten Tomatoes score that you can apply to what critics think of a thing, but it also contains a User Score that's often the inverse of what the algorithm offers up. We live in a time where everyone feels the need to put a number, a score, on every piece of art. It's not new.

You do a gigantic film. What a cool moment. What a random slice of life that you find inspiring and magical. Then you return back to the talent pool of everyone that could be cast in any kind of movie or TV show.

I stumbled into an independent picture next. I don't see indie film as anything less grand than gigantic studio pictures, but outsiders might look in and ask "What happened to your career?" My career continued. That's all that matters. Your ship remains afloat. Whether you're riding the seven seas or sailing down a small river, you're still on the journey. And in the process of staying afloat, you travel to so many new places.

This is how I wound up landing on the shores of a film called *But I'm A Cheerleader.*

You don't know what a script will blossom into You can recognize a film that connects with you, and then hope that it will connect with others. That hope leads you to choose projects that make the most impact. You read a script and you have a flicker of intuition that this might matter. You sign up, and believe in the collective goal that everyone on set strives towards, but you're not too worried about what happens after the credits roll. You're there to live in the moment as an actor.

So at first, this was just a movie I took on. *But I'm A Cheerleader* was another mountain I chose to climb. I appreciate that I don't see projects from faraway, but from the inside of the work.

The film starred, Natasha Lyonne, Clea Duvall, and RuPaul, alongside Melanie Lapinski, Doug Spain, Kip Purdue, Joel Michaely, and Kate Towne, who ended up being my best friend for the next 10 years. And directed by Jamie Babbit. When I look back at that cast, it was a smash of the coolest, most talented kids from my generation of young Hollywood. So for anyone that thought, at the time, that this was a step down for me...you know...suck it?

I'm honored to have been part of this cult classic LGBTQ+ film before the term "LGBTQ" was popularized in the mainstream. For me, it was the first time I played a gay character in a film. I remember going in for the audition and being like, "What am I doing here? I'm not gay." There's tons of gay actors that could play the role. I acknowledged that I was filling a representational position that I did not deserve, similar to playing a Native American character as a kid. Or anything else I played around that time, when Hollywood couldn't distinguish between one brown kid and the next. Why would they come to me to play a gay character? Not because I was uncomfortable in the role, but because I understood the experience of what gay actors must have similarly struggled with when they tried to find their footing in the industry. I didn't want to take this from anyone. I didn't want anyone to resent me for making these choices.

Also, the character's name is Dolph, right? When you read the original script, Dolph is supposed to be the quarterback of the football team. Blond, blue-eyed, six-foot-something. The Golden Boy. He ended up as a wrestler rather than a quarterback by my suggestion, but I was still weirded out by the Ken doll casting call. Then director Jamie Babbit talked to me and I asked why on Earth she wanted me to take this character. She goes, "It's because he's the Boy Next Door, Dante, just the same as you."

I loved her for that. I love her for that to this day. That moment changed everything for me. It's when my old concerns fell away from me, and I felt myself rise above the standards by which we judge this shit.

She saw me, you know? Not my ethnicity, but the essence of that character.

The boy next door.

Around this, some studio executives were doubtful. They wouldn't say it to my face, but they didn't believe that I was that kind of wholesome. And I confronted them. I said that they should go to their neighborhood and look around their block. To actually look at their neighbors beyond a passing glance. I bet the Boy Next Door looks like me.

I went to Sundance for the first time with *But I'm a Cheerleader*. Early Sundance, that was true indie filmmaking. Nowadays indie filmmaking is lower-budget studio stuff, as opposed to real shoestring cinema. My memory of that time is so beautiful. The film is still a staple within the LGBTQ+ community. It's funny and poignant, and many kids have told me that it's helped them come out to their parents. To be part of a moment like that in someone's life is a true honor.

At the time, I was worried about how the world would react. The year 1999 was a different era. The acceptance of sexuality as a spectrum was certainly on the rise, but it was still a far cry from how open the world is today. Then there was, to a lesser degree, the thought that this would impact my professional career, because casting directors were often devoid of the sort of awareness I hoped they could possess. I questioned if Hollywood would see me as another "type" after this film, the way they only saw my ethnicity at the start of my career. If there was any part of me that didn't want to be defined as a gay character actor, it wasn't from a place of homophobia, but an awareness of the prejudice structural to the industry. It was me recognizing that I shouldn't take those roles from the actors who deserved them. The third was, of course, what would my more conservative family members think when they saw this? Would they see it purely as the work, or would they be upset by the content?

I hope I'm an actor who presents honesty in all that he does. I do the work, and my work is often deciding how to share a character in a way that translates the most grounded, human version of who they are. So. This was that moment of panic over whether I was the right person to convey the mere action of a boy-on-boy kiss. Even with that, I was confident in myself and my skill set. I was in a place where I welcomed whatever life would bring. I'd done plenty of stage-kiss work, but I didn't want to sell this experience short by pretending they were all the same. I wanted it to have my attention, and my respect.

Within the film, I would kiss Kip Pardue. I don't know if you've seen Kip Pardue, but he is one of the most attractive human beings to ever descend from Mount Olympus. I mean, I am calling into question his status as a terrestrial being. Again, post-casting announcement, there were so many moments where awe was all I could express. I was cast as the boy next door, which was a breakthrough for me. I was cast in a non-straight role, which was good for me but better for the industry. But Kip as my boyfriend was the biggest turn of all. In a traditional casting situation, Kip would be the jock hero and I'd be playing the dweeby Asian guy from down the street. Those roles were reversed here. I was this jock hero and Kip Pardue was my dorky boyfriend. It's the type of choice that felt boundary pushing at the time, but twenty years later in 2019 would still be inventive.

We made a pact, Kip and I, to kiss for the first time on-screen. We rehearsed right up to that point. We studied each other. And what we shot that first take became what you see in the film. If I'm going to step into the shoes of someone else's experience, the least I could do was be completely honest to that experience. And that's what we did in *But I'm a Cheerleader*.

The Debut came out in 2001, a few years later. I played Ben, a kid who just wants to be an artist. Sound familiar?

The Debut was the first Hollywood film about Filipinos. Ever. I mean, maybe not ever ever. But ostensibly: ever.

Right now, Asian Americans have the most positive profile we've had in America. The highest we've ever been. The Debut was 19 years ago, and it took a generation to get to anything resembling Crazy Rich Asians. That's progress. Glacial, but moving, and I want to be hopeful. We're finally getting heard on our own terms, and our stories are coming alive on the national stage. Our American story.

The Debut was the first time I got to play Filipino. At that point, I was 21 or 22 and I'd played everything. So many different kinds of Asian: Chinese, Cambodian, Korean, alongside all sorts of Latino roles. Finally, I could be a face for the Fil-Am community on the Hollywood screen, and my brother and sister and cousin were all in the film, too. It was incredible to see my family members on film, but it wasn't just us. I could see my grandmother's smile in my brother's face, the gait of our mom in my sister. Our parents and grandparents, our ancestors, all the traits and culture we inherited— all of these people and journeys were in the movie, too.

It was fascinating because I'd worked so closely with my brothers, and we'd studied together for years in the same acting school. They're all accomplished actors in their own right, and to be able to work with them and travel to set together was so fun, and illuminating. We share the same history of studying theatre, but everyone has their own process of creating characters. We each had our style. Darion played the antagonist in the movie, and we had several days of fighting. We grew up as brothers, and to bring that brotherly competition to the screen in a positive way helped push everybody to the next level.

It felt a bit like cheating. We made it easy for the filmmakers because what direction did you need to give actors that have already spent a decade sparring? Maybe it's not cheating per se, but it could have been harder. How much of that do you choose to reveal to the world, especially in your younger years? Knowing what you know about your family? How much do you want to go there? There's a balance to every situation. My brothers know when I'm faking it. And they'll call me. You can't fake anything if you're entering that space together. You go in entirely, or you don't do it all. But that's not to say it can't be fun. It's all within play. That's just how filmmaking works: every project is its own puzzle. You go about every day trying to put the pieces together. Part of the problem is that we don't know what the final picture will be. Hopefully it resolves as an aesthetically pleasing solution. Or at least a work of art that challenges others to do better.

Every time you create a new project, you build a new village and family. The whole squad comes together, and you go through life and death situations that only you guys as a cast and crew will experience in the production of this show. *The Debut* was such a special cast, and a really special time in my life. I didn't really grow up on Filipino cinema, but when I worked with some of these stars, I could feel the truth of who they were through their work.

Folks like Eddie Garcia, who'd been working for decades and decades at that time in Filipino cinema. He passed away recently, and I hold my memories of him so close to my heart. It was such a privilege to just know him, let alone work alongside one of the greatest actors of all time. When you have that much experience, you carry that same weight as the big American star do. It's not just audience perception, it's visceral.

Actors of color rarely get that chance in America, because we don't get the lead roles in projects. We're not even considered, most times. In many ways, seeing Eddie act with a confidence grown outside of the American studio system — that's what influenced me later on to be a part of the Asian American movement to create media, to create opportunities. I see what's possible when I work with these actors. If "traditional" Hollywood won't give us space, we will build our own set. I want to give the next generation a real shot. So *The Debut* has continued to be important in my life, long after the last scene. I'm so happy that it's become an important film to the Asian American community, and more specifically the Filipino American community. For better or worse, it's the one Fil-Am film everybody in the Philippines owns.

I'm proud to be a part of that, but by the same token, there should be more. It guides my work today as a filmmaker, helping to inspire Asian Americans to make those— because it's not enough. That was eighteen, twenty years ago. We should fill the sky with our own stars.

It's nice to be in a place to hire the same people that helped bring me up. Around the start of a new film I'm directing, I sat down with Tirso Cruz III, who played my father in *The Debut*. We were in the Philippines. It still felt like a family reunion. You cross paths with so many people over the years. A lot of people you work with over the years and you cross paths again. There's guys that want to or have hired me for things, and vice versa now. I get to make space for someone that I truly admire, and love. It feels great. It's the cycle of this industry and I'm grateful to work with such inspirational people. As I'm putting together my film, I want the best folks I can on my project.

Again, this isn't to say that work with family isn't A Lot.

Everything is personal in the arts. Some days become therapy sessions. Part of the craft becomes processing your stuff in front of a packed room, which isn't always the most comfortable thing to do. But that's part of the gig: in one way or another, working things out in front of an audience. It could be the world, or a few people on set, or your own reflection as you memorize lines in front of a mirror. That intimacy still has positive sides. These are the people closest to me in my life, and I get to see them grow as artists. When they do something brilliant, I get to be one of the people there to see it, and applaud their level-up.

Yet sometimes, the work can be too personal. Secrets are revealed and used against you, becoming a stain on your growth and relationships in your life outside the acting world. That's horrible, and I've seen it happen personally to myself and my family members. We've competed our whole lives, and we continue to audition against each other. When we were young, we didn't really comprehend that relationship, and how the business works. We felt that in order to succeed, the ones we loved the most had to fail. That feeling isn't necessarily true, but digesting it as a young artist is hard. Later, you realize you're not in competition with anyone but yourself.

My brothers auditioned for Rufio in *Hook*. It's funny to look back now and see how things panned out, but at the same time, it's a real piece of our personal history. Who knows? I came out on one side, but I have a certain perspective. I'm sure if you talked to each brother, we'd all have different perspectives on our individual relationships. Four brothers in the same industry, auditioning for the same roles. Everyone's feeling their worst half the time, with so much comparison to the successes and failures of their brothers. That's not fair, but tons of theatrical families have managed throughout the years. Over the decades, we've been able to use our successes to strengthen the family tree, as it were. Use that energy it to move forward together, rather than degrade each other.

My siblings are all in the industry, but they've spread far beyond our starting point. They're still actors, as well as producers and writers. It's rare for us to wind up in that competitive place we once were. While the Basco Brothers spent decades in competition, no one puts us in the same casting room these days. That's good for us. It's new. It means we aren't at each other's throats. We would've kept that up, we got good at it. But thirty years in, who needs to continue that brawl?

I think what we've realized is that everyone's become accomplished in their own right. We've all traveled around, and gotten to see what each of us has done. We're different types — we could be up for the same role, but if they want Dante, they want Dante. If they want Dion, they want lively and witty. Life has blessed us so much, and everyone has found victories along the way. When you're younger, brothers are really tight. It's like being born into a boy band. We've been that way since birth. Yet for all that these relationships nurtured me, I can't forget my sister always felt like an outsider compared to the brothers. She's not one of the boys, she's her own thing.

There were years that the brothers didn't talk to our parents, didn't talk to our sister. Years when we reconciled— there's a certain codependency with the brothers because of that package deal. With my sister, she went to New York and grew into her own person. There's a freedom there that I had to learn for myself. With us brothers, everyone put us in a lane, and we adhered— "I'll just be this guy." It's a beautiful, how we complement each other, but part of life's adventure is learning your own definition of what it means to be human.

That codependency is so fascinating. When I stopped seeing my brothers every day, I recognized that I've leaned on them for my entire life. As an adult, I realized there were basic parts of my personality and humanity that I had to catch-up on real quick, or I was gonna have a rough time. I ended up moving out of the house to see who I was alone, outside of my brothers. I developed other skills, and traveled the world. But, listen — we're Filipino, and close-knit family circles are part of the culture. Right now, all of my brothers live in the same compound. Even my sister had some kids and moved back home. I'm the black sheep that goes out on my own. And that said, I'm just three miles away.

When I meet up with everyone over a holiday, and crack a beer and talk about the old days— there's this question of whether we have to reevaluate our past: is there any resentment there, or just a really heavy emotional blanket? We talk about it. We've lived the lives of artists. A circus life. You must reach for things beyond yourself. With that comes compromise, especially in our childhoods. We left our hometown and friends to pursue this larger-than-life Hollywood dream, with no assurance that it would work for us. How ludicrous it all was, how lucky we were to find our paths regardless.

We talk about how acting school hurt as much as it helped us. The damage that caused us as individuals. Even though I think we've grown past it, it's part of our family history. If nothing else, it's brought up to remind us not to lose focus of what's important. When you're young and in pursuit of this dream, it feels more important than anything. You need to be obsessed with success in order to be successful. It's not regular. You've got to sacrifice a lot. People come to me with their kids and ask for advice, because I was a kid actor. I'm like, "This is the deal, it's almost like being an athlete. You train every day, and there's no promise of winning."

No one forced us into the industry. My parents supported us, but I don't think they really knew what we were doing. They do know that it worked out. And if your kid wants to be a basketball player, you don't have to tell him to play basketball. Guess what? You're gonna wake up, and your kid will be on the court, because that's what he wants to do. Same thing with us, we'd be on the dance floor, breakdancing. Wake up, eat, dance. Whatever it was, it's always been in us. You've got to do the work and hone your craft, but that drive? That was already in me. Parents can really push you far, even when you're a kid and it's the thing you want to do— at some point, kids rebel and push back on that. If my mom had been a Dance Mom and I were a competitive dancer, at some point in high school I would have broken, and sworn I'd never dance again. It's a strange gift, that they never understood what we were trying to do. They just loved, and supported.

I remember waking up my dad in San Francisco like "We've got to get to acting class." That was me. That was all of us. That built us to the place where we could all work on screen together, to have these skill sets that complemented each other. In that way, *The Debut* holds up a mirror for the world to see us. Or at least a lens to see us through. It's a movie, but it's us on the screen. And for it to be one of the biggest Filipino American breakthrough features of all time — it's a good look.

The Debut keeps us frozen in that moment of history. How we fought, and loved. And the next generation can see what this once looked like: the moment we know that more was possible.

Sometimes we say things that just aren't true
like "I'd never do that" or "I'd die without you."
"I'd never move to the suburbs."
"I'd never date an Asian guy."
"If I couldn't eat sushi, I would just die."
"I'd never be caught dead in anything but a Mercedes-Benz."
"I could never love a girl if I hate all her friends."
It's like Republicans saying how Democrats are liberal

or
Democrats saying that Republicans are evil.
Now I grew up a little bit, I can admit it's a bunch of bull.
See,
first thing: you don't die.
You just don't die. You don't.
I didn't talk to my parents for seven years of my life
two people I love most in life, but
nobody died, we just didn't talk.
Forgot about the love, held onto the grudge and
I ain't gonna lie, there were a lot of melancholy nights, but
a lot of days too filled with
laughter and smiles on faces.
My family will always regard those days as
the dark ages
but what I'm trying to say is
the boundaries we have
are the boundaries we make.
We constantly enforce them by the negative things that we say.
Everything you say,
I can give you an example
of the exact opposite being true,
we limit ourselves to our point of view.
You
you
you argue
Who cares if you're right?
Does it matter if you're living a miserable life?
This life is filled with infinite possibilities
I'm not just up here
talking down on you,
waxing philosophy
cause yo
yo, I'm probably gonna move to the suburbs,

that could be cool.
Don't lie, you might move there too.
I'm just saying,
don't know so much.
Leave room to be surprised.
Every now and then,
if you're like,
"Man, I think I'm out my head"
Chances are
You ain't really living life.

INTO THE FIRE NATION

One of my first jobs as a voice actor was a tire commercial. I wasn't sure how to play it, because it was so cheesy. It was a tire talking to another tire. The first tire asks "How are you feeling?" The other tire responds with "A little flat."

Yeah. So.

The work looks like that on certain days. We all have rent. When you're in Hollywood, there are different avenues to get a check cut. The avenue everyone knows is movies and television, but the other avenues are commercials, print, all of these sub-levels. Scientology hires a lot of actors into industrials, which are training films for different industries. You can figure out how and why they engage in that. I've done some, not for Scientology, but for Disney and in-house things for other corporations. Everyone kind of knew about voice-over, but in the last ten years or so, it's gotten more attention. Thanks to Seth Mac-Farlane, all of a sudden, voice-over has become a sought-after profession. Nowadays, I get stopped all the time because of my voice acting career. People are like, "I want to be a voice actor. That's all I want to do."

Well, let's agree that it's the best version of Hollywood: if you gain five pounds, no one cares. You don't have to put on a costume, you come in and do what you do. It's not something I ever thought about, let alone valued, before it came into the mainstream. Not that I devalued it. When you're an actor, you want to diversify. You don't want that one small lane. The people making their living solely off of s are a) brilliant, and b) limited in number.

My first V.O. was a few lines in *A Goofy Movie*.

That sometimes gets a strong reaction out of people. The kind where they shout "Are you kidding me?" I get why. It's a part of your childhood and once again I just happen to be there. Me, Dante, the tween phantom.

That's one of the weird bonuses of V.O. Folks will always be shocked by where you showed up. In *A Goofy Movie* I say, "Yo, Stacy! Talk to me, talk to me, talk to me, ba-byyy!" People that love *A Goofy Movie* know that line, and know that it's me — someone even made a t-shirt of it.

I've been on lists for Disney auditions, for everything from *Lion King* to *Mulan*. I never booked any of those roles. When you're auditioning professionally, you go out a few times a week. You do your best, and they either like you or they don't.

Years went by before voice-acting really took off for me. Then, Cartoon Network had a new pilot, called *A Kitty Bobo Show*. There were Asian American writers who had me in mind while writing it. I went in and got the role. I wasn't even represented as a voice actor at the time, but a friend from acting class, Chad Dorrick was like, "You should come to William-Morris." I signed just for V.O. Someone reps my voice, someone reps my theatrical stuff, someone reps my commercials, then a manager oversees everything. You might even have a hosting agent, if someone wants you to host on E!, something on MTV— back in those days you had that, and a lawyer, and maybe a public relations person who got X amount of money every month.

At some point I had upward of ten hyper-specific reps.

That was, you know, not quite sustainable. Now big agencies take over the smaller facets of the industry. It's fewer cooks in the kitchen, but it's still about managing the division of labor. You're basically the CEO of a company, and that company is you as a person.

In the world of voice-over auditions, you go into an office, and you read all kinds of different characters. The room at WME has a big group of actors, both onscreen and V.O. There's a huge lobby where I got to know them over the years. Actors, trading actor stories. Coming from on-screen acting, where every relationship can feel so intense, it was cool to see the camaraderie of voice actors. Some of them I'm friends with to this day, fifteen, twenty years later. One by one, we'd go in the booth and do our thing. At WME, sometimes there'll be 20-30 people in the lobby, and you could be waiting there for over an hour, easy.

When they don't get the job, many actors take it to heart. I understand why. It feels like the essence of you is being rejected. For some reason, voice-acting isn't taken as personally. You're playing a tiger. A dolphin. A kid with fire powers. After on-camera auditions, it would be easy to carry an anger with you, that they didn't like how *you* looked. You can internalize that, whereas with V.O. it's simply the sound of your voice. There will be other roles. You can move on, change your tone.

Then again, there are fewer people in the V.O. world. You work on so many projects together that you're not pigeonholed into typecasting nearly as much. I came in with some history, a decent actor with a decent background, but all of a sudden I started booking roles I never thought I could get.

I'd come off a Disney pilot called *The Chang Family Saves The World*, a show about an Asian American family that discovers they have superpowers. It was directed by Paris Barclay, and produced and created by John Ridley, who later won an Oscar for *12 Years A Slave*. But that show didn't go anywhere. We got the pilot, the trades picked us up, *Variety* predicted we were good to go. At the last second, ABC pulled it from the slate. Which was a bummer. Then somehow, I got this show on Disney. *American Dragon* was the first series I booked for them.

It was basically the same show as *The Chang Family Saves The World*, I just turned into a cartoon dragon. Jake Long is getting a lot of love again. There's an army of Disney-ites all over the world who remind me that I was an original Disney character. Not only that, but the first Asian American hero for Disney, which is a pretty big deal.

This brings me to the audition for *Avatar: The Last Airbender*.

Me and Mae Whitman, who played my love interest Rose in *Jake Long*—we both had auditions at Nickelodeon. Mine was for *Avatar*. When you go to Nickelodeon Studios in Burbank, the whole building had green slime on it. You walk through the gates and you see these murals of Spongebob, CatDog, it's great.

They gave me a script, and concept art of something you'd never recognize as *Avatar: The Last Airbender* now.

It was obviously Asian-inspired with marital arts and elements, and a character with a nasty scar on his face. I thought to myself, this ain't Nickelodeon at all. I just didn't believe that it would go forward.

There may be a handful of things that I'd do every year for Cartoon Network or Nickelodeon, shorts and pilots, and most of them never saw the light of a television screen. You work, you get paid for the day, and hopefully you get to see it when it's done. I didn't think too much of it, same as all the other auditions.

Voice-acting, and *Avatar* in particular, taught me that no matter my expectations, sometimes I have to walk through any open door I see. The future can be better than anything I could've planned. Getting to be an integral part of a new fairytale? Amazing. Fulfilling my wildest fantasies.

People always ask whether I prefer voice-over or on-screen acting. It's all performance to me. Whether captured by a camera or just a microphone, the character must step with you. With Zuko, I was a thirty-year-old man playing a fifteen-year-old boy. I've played a teen more than a dozen times in my career. At a certain level, I know what it feels like. I've done it in life, and I've done it on-screen. That's all that acting is, striving for the truth in every moment.

I quickly realized *Avatar* wasn't the normal Nickelodeon thing. This was more mature and complicated. Animation is so tricky. You look at the page, full of mysteries to solve. When you do voice-over, you're not going to see the final product for years. It's not like a regular TV show where we shoot, and it'll be out in a few weeks. Nope. When you're doing it originally, it's just lines on a page. You're reciting a story with other actors, and acting scenes out.

For most of the recordings, I was in a studio with everyone else. None of us would see the episode for, like, two years. We did our jobs: to be mindful within every syllable of the script. You just come in and let it go. We had no idea that *Avatar* would be so important.

Even after the show came out, I still had no idea that it connected with people so deeply. I never even saw any episodes as
they aired. I went to the premiere, and thought it was awesome,
but I wasn't watching a lot of animation at the time in general.

It wasn't until I shot *Take The Lead* that I had any clue. I remember leaving the set one day with Antonio Banderas, and
he asked what else I was up to. I said I had a thing to do for a
cartoon in the States, and he was so happy to chat with another
voice actor. I was like, "Yeah. You're Puss in Boots. I know who
you are." We had this whole talk about voice acting, and I was
so alarmed by how much they got paid for *Shrek*. He was like,
"Can you believe they paid me that for two days of work?" I
was like, "Um. No, I can't believe that. I love that you're putting
me and you together in this voice acting world, that's something
else we have in common. But I am not on your level. Nope."

I love him. He was so nice, saying we were both voice actors
like that and I was like, "We sure are, Antonio."

I didn't think anyone else knew about my show, but one of
the other actors on the movie, Brandon Andrews—he was 22
at the time, he wasn't a kid—was like, "Hey dude, what are
you doing?" I said I going to go do my series, a little cartoon in
LA, *Avatar: The Last Airbender*. I saw his eyes pop open as he
shouted, "What? What are you talking about? That's my show!
Who are you?"

"Prince Zuko."

"WHAT?"

He freaked out— a grown guy freaking out about a cartoon
we do for twelve-year-olds. So that's how far outside of the animation world I was, even as I did that gig. I was so surprised!
I invited him to the studio to watch me do one of the episodes
remotely, from Toronto. It was like I'd taught him how to bend
lightning, he was so excited.

At Sundance that year, I ran into Jason Isaacs, who plays General Shao on the show. I knew Jason from *Avatar*, and I'm a fan of *Harry Potter* and *The Patriot*. He's a dope actor, and a cool guy to be around. We ran into each other in the snow, and he turned around like, "Dante. DANTE. That fucking cartoon we did, can you fucking believe it?"

We were tripping about how it had became this phenomenal hit. This little cartoon that we both didn't think about too much, became this big impactful show people lost their minds over. I had no idea it would get such a response.

Then people started bowing to me in public. That was a new thing for me.

Wild as it is to get used to something like that, I am. It's weird because my voice is synonymous with Zuko. Even though he doesn't look like me, it's still me.

Ultimately, it serves as a microcosm of voice-acting in Hollywood for me. I didn't think that skill would impact my life so much in the last decade and a half. The character of Zuko, I didn't think much of him. Joke's on me: it's one of the biggest characters of my career, and influenced my life in a way I never imagined. We don't know anything. Yeah, I've been around town for a long time and I've given advice, but there are things we just don't know.

So there was a buzz around *Avatar*. It's hard to think of life before social media — I didn't even do Comic Con much. It wasn't what it is now. There were long lines, but it was just cool and weird. That period of time when I didn't have social media was interesting: I couldn't obsess over how people reacted to me. It's wild to think what my Rufio life would have been like if social media was around when *Hook* came out. I imagine I'd be a much different person.

Without social media, my progression up the ladder was much slower. As an Asian actor, it's always been a conversation with management and agents. I have friends who are white actors, who audition for forty or fifty shows. When you're an actor of color, those auditions aren't nearly as frequent. Asians get the lowest of the low roles. I may go out for three, maybe up to five pilots a season. It's limited, but I'm also selective. My whole career has been doing roles that aren't Asian roles, they just happened to be Asian because I was the one doing them. If I read the pages and they demean a group of people or set anybody back, I'm out.

So *Avatar: The Last Airbender* ran for a couple of years, and it ended. Now it has this incredible legacy, where it matters so much more now than when it ran, and it was pretty beloved when it first aired. Every year it seems like the fandom gets bigger. I wonder if this is the Dante brand? "I'll make a bunch of stuff and what was once a cult following has become mainstream and a big deal, and I'll become more famous after I've done it." I don't know how any of this works. When you have a chance to do something, you try to do it really well. Whether you have the good fortune that people actually give a shit about anything you do, I don't know. You've got to be in the moment, and do the best with what you can do, and hope for the best. By the same token, you can't be connected to that success either, you don't have any control over that.

You work on all of these things, and by the very nature of you working on them, the project employs hundreds, if not thousands of people. Now that I'm a producer, I think more about those animators and crew that my work enabled to have careers. I'm aware of the people that we hire for my indie films. I grew up in the industry, so acting to me isn't just the people you see onscreen. It's never been. I have a very close relationship with the wardrobe people, and the makeup and hair people, and the PAs running around, and all the stunt people and gaffers and grips, cracking jokes with the people in charge of cameras and lighting. To this day, we take bets on what the light meter will to read.

I'm a blue-collar actor that works with blue-collar people. You're hanging with these folks for weeks, months. You're traveling with these people. There are friendships being made. There's the A-list part of the crew, the producers and yeah, there's a high-end dinner here and there. But there's so much regular stuff, like sitting by craft services talking football. You're all working on something like *Avatar*. You make it over a couple of years. And then there's a live-action film.

People ask about my thoughts on that. I don't have many. I bet you can guess where I stand. What are your feelings on that?

With the film, we all auditioned for it. Or not all—I know Mae Whitman did, Jack De Sena, myself. I thought Jack almost got hired for a hot second. I never even got to meet M. Night, I'm sure he had his own ideas going on. I know there were tons of people going up to bat for me to play the role, but things happen. It's Hollywood. You can't control what happens.

I never saw the film. The shows means so much to me, and I didn't hear a lot of great things about the movie, even within the Avatar family. I'll probably end up watching it sometime, with fans maybe.

Folks were upset with the film, and I want to clarify that it's hard to make a movie, period. How many actual good movies came out last year? M. Night might've made some mistakes but nobody's perfect. I don't want to alienate M. Night Shyamalan, I think he's a great director. Nobody can get every thing right.

Personally, I can't say anything because I never saw the movie, but I wrote a blog about it when it was coming out. Fans asked me about it, and the blog went pretty viral, about whitewashing Hollywood. I grew up in the Hollywood system, I did *Hook* as a person of color, but Rufio was a white character that I ended up booking. When you get that platform, I know how that changes the trajectory of your career. The reality is that there are tons of young white roles in Hollywood. But when it's a person of color, especially Asian, whitewashing ruins the opportunity to give the next kid— maybe someone like me— a chance to build their career. That has ramifications beyond a resume. The film missed the chance to uplift Asian kids as fully-rounded characters. As role models.

So much of that movie is stepping backwards, from a director who also isn't white. In some ways, my legacy was walked back a few steps. But I'm aware there are so many things that happen with money people and studios. It's hard to speak on someone else's process and what happens.

A lot of stuff did not go right. I was mad when I heard that they were going to cast Jesse McCartney as Prince Zuko. That pissed me off in the sense that it's just crazy. When they got Dev Patel, I was like, "Okay, he's a dope actor, he's Indian, it is what it is." *Slumdog Millionaire* had just gotten an Oscar. He's obviously a great call for that character, a super talented actor. But with the few pictures I saw of Dev on set, I thought about that day in *Hook* when Spielberg approved my costume, and I was immediately concerned. Even in the finished product, Dev looks like he's thinking "I shouldn't be in these clothes and no I don't want to be in them and nothing here is working."

People expect me to be very angry about the film. I have a good level of disconnect from my work, but that balance can be hard. You've got to care enough to perform your best but at the end of the day, it's not precious.

When we shot *The Debut*, me and the director went back and forth about how a scene should go. I wanted to do it one way and he'd want another, and that's just the process. It's passionate. But after all is said and done, you have no control over what other people think of your work. It is what it is. It's something you did, a piece of you. If that encapsulates that moment in your life, then that's cool. But what else can you do?

In the V.O. world, I've gotten to expand this work into innumerable little parts in TV shows and video games. I was in skating games, and a *Terminator* movie tie-in, and an adaptation of *Scarface*. I'm in *Mortal Kombat*. I know that I freak out about the various intellectual properties that Dante Basco is a permanent fixture in at this point, like *Peter Pan* and *Avatar*, but I'm in *Mortal Kombat*. The '90s kid in me thinks that rips.

I'm also in a game called *Def Jam: Fight For New York*. I barely remember recording that. It was in 2004 and it was a fighting game with the rappers of the Def Jam label. This one comes up sometimes now, because the game is having a resurgence in the world of competitive fighting games. It's another one of those Classic Dante Moments, where I touch a creative work and it becomes a cult favorite.

It isn't the worst curse.

As part of that *Terminator: Salvation* game, my only big memories are of spending entire days shouting. Shouting about grenades being thrown. Shouting about an attack. I had an even worse session for a Vietnam-era title. We had helicopters going the whole session, where I had to do all the cues — over a hundred cues — over a helicopter sound. Like we're in war. You have the helicopter chopping the whole time, with every line, every grunt, everyone yelling for four hours straight. I couldn't speak for two days after that.

This was the kind of work that forced a strike in the Screen Actors Guild last year, as V.O. performers realized they had to slash their vocal chords for work like this without proper protection and compensation.

You've got to take care of your voice, your instrument. You have to pad the actors the right way so we're not damaging ourselves. V.O. actors are still actors. On-screen actors can receive residual payments after their original work, for things like reruns and streaming. It's not always the same with V.O. The companies should share some of the residual payment with us. They're not all hits, but there are some games I've been a part of that have sold over 100 million dollars. It's not that we need to get everything, but like any actor, catching residuals is part of a fair contract.

I've taken vocal lessons and speech classes, and I blew my voice out a lot. Still blow it out sometimes. The best advice is to just warm up, which any vocal class will teach you. "Yellow leather," "Toy boat, toy boat, toy boat," stuff to get your enunciation. From there, you've got to really know the script. You're going to get emotional, you've got to prepare for it. Know when you're going to hit those beats. Use your diaphragm. Make your choices and be in the moment, but even then, you have to know what you're doing with your instrument or all of a sudden, you start screaming and crying out of nowhere and blow your voice out.

I try to always stand up in the recording studio so I have energy when I'm acting. You have headphones on most of the time, because you're listening to yourself and whatever's happening in the booth. But I usually have one ear off, so I can hear what I actually sound like. I don't know if I'm projecting into the microphone or not, I'm just trying to concentrate on the acting.

To end my tales from the voice work world, let me tell you when V.O. work really blew me away: my day with Mark Hamill.

In the first season of *Avatar*, I had a scene with my father Ozai. I usually did the whole episode with the rest of the cast, but the manager said it was just me and my father today. It was a rainy afternoon in Burbank, and in comes this guy wearing all black.

Andrea Romano, a legendary voice-over director, introduced Mark Hamill as my dad. I swear the door opened by itself, and mist flooded in, and he floated across the room. And we went straight to the scene. Ozai and I were fighting, just before he scars me. I shouted lines like, "Father, no!" Which is weird to say to Mark Hamill, the ultimate son.

The young *Star Wars* fan inside me — who spent hours with my brothers, arguing over who was Luke and Han Solo, fighting with makeshift lightsabers in the garage— screamed. If you recall this episode, it's not just any fight: it's the Agni Kai. We both immediately turn into martial arts masters and firebenders of the highest order, with all these Matrix-like moves...well, kind of, just vocally, you know? I mean, we're voice actors.

And we're in this battle! My father Ozai is imposing all his power on me, and Zuko fights with all his strength but ultimately gets defeated. And, to further prove his point, Ozai scars Zuko, leaving him with a burn on his face. We were in the booth making enough sounds for a thousand Kung Fu masters, the gasps and grunts of landing deadly blows, and receiving them. I wanted to prove that I could meet him at his level.

I wanted to prove that I was on equal footing with Mark Hamill.

Stop laughing.

We did all that, and then it ended, and he floated back out on the mist in his black getup.

I crumpled into my chair, spent from a fairly demanding scene with one of the greatest voice actors in town, and a personal hero of mine since childhood.

As I looked at the glass to Andrea smiling back at me, the moment burned into me, this moment I'll never forget. Matter of fact, I might embellish a bit as I tell the story for history books. But there I was, in one of the most surreal moments of my life. Essentially, I got to play out the Luke-Vader scene from *Star Wars: The Empire Strikes Back*, the scene where Luke gets his hand cut off by his vengeful father Darth Vader. Except in this alternate universe, I was Luke Skywalker and Mark Hamill was Darth Vader.

I don't know if it gets any better than that. This is definitely one of the reasons why kids come to Hollywood. It's one of the reasons I did.

He's such a brilliant actor. He has so much range in his voice. In between takes, he was just in the room reading a newspaper, a real newspaper. His comic book collection is probably worth millions of dollars. He holds a key place in Americana and the fandom worlds, with an encyclopedia of Hollywood history behind him. When we talked, he was as excited about his all-time version of the Joker as doing *Amadeus* on Broadway.

"Okay, I'm up with Robin Williams, doing my day job with Mark Hamill." I'm always opposite the hero, but the hero I'm opposite is a forever meta-hero to everyone in the world. It's a precarious footing to hold, but perhaps the standing that will become my legacy.

Unless that sounds ridiculous.

I'm fine with that. You have to be proud of yourself sometimes.

POETICS

You may have noticed by now that I care about poetry. Not just care, but I prefer to express myself in that way. The language of poetry is the language of me. Is "the language of me" a bit clumsy? Figures. This isn't my preference. If I could talk to you purely through the medium of poetry, this book would be a much different adventure. Direct in a different way, but perhaps a series of undecipherable metaphors that would, as a result, have made this complicated for everyone else.

You would have understood. At this point, I know you would have.

Poetry matters to me. That shouldn't be a line that differentiates me from others. We should live in a world where everyone unabashedly loves poetry. I don't know how we wound up here, where I'm an outlier. I'll proudly claim it. And I proudly claim what comes by extension.

Time to tell you about Da Poetry Lounge.

Alongside Shihan Van Clief, Gimel Hooper, and Poetri, I founded a venue for poetry. This brings me such joy. Plenty of folks I know can brag about a plane, or a dispensary, or a production company. *Dante, what did you sink your finances into?* Well, a poetry venue. *Is that a wise investment?* Oh, hell no. But it's one that I believe in. I believe in poetry, and I believe in the people behind poetry and I believe in spackling the void of poetry in pop culture.

I want to fix it. I want to reclaim it. I'm here to believe in what has been abandoned.

My oldest brother Derek was into poetry when I was younger, he read loads of Pablo Neruda. I was super impacted by *Dead Poets Society*, and by all those transcendental poets. I studied their work. Then in acting classes, our coach at the time had us recite poems in between scenes. So we did scenes from *Romeo and Juliet*, romantic stuff, and then Charles Bukowski for intermission. I loved Diane Wakoski, and hip-hop and rap— it's all poetry.

Then we started rapping. Me and my brothers wrote verses, and in 1993 we went to an open mic in La Brea called the Yaya Tea Bar, where I met Roni of Backstreet Poetry. We stayed the entire night. I came back the next weekend and ended up onstage with a harmonica, and read my first poem there. Roni became my mentor in the poetry world— I hung out with her a lot. I ended up meeting my partner Shihan at the open mic. That friendship birthed our poetry venue. I started going to a club called Blase Blah, and I walked in and— matter of fact, before that, there were these girls. These Latina girls did a night on Melrose called Fly Mamis, and it was hosted by Chris Spencer, so he asked me in the middle of the night, "Can you come and do poetry?"

I said yeah, and we tagged it Dante's Poetry Night in the middle of the Fly Mamis. I brought a poet and he killed it. So we brought that to Blase Blah, and then it just got so packed at Blase Blah, with Poetry Lounge coming in at midnight for a set.

I just turned it into my own venue.

I started inviting people to come over to my house, which got packed. From there, it went to sandwich shops, which got packed. My friend Ted Firestone owned a theater, Zoo Theater, that got packed. Every venue we went to burst with verses and finger snaps by dawn. We've been in the Greenway Court Theatre on Fairfax since 2000. The name has evolved from Dante's Poetry Lounge, to Da's Poetry Lounge, to simply Da Poetry Lounge. The energy of every open mic is as invigorating as the first time I stepped onstage with a poem.

There's so much I discover in poetry that I can't find anywhere else. When you're acting in a movie, you're a character in someone else's story, which is fine. But poetry was my first avenue into writing. It's my chance to tell my own story. It gave me the ability to digest my life.

It's a better reflection of how I feel than prose. I'm definitely a poet. I just think lyrically, I lean into poetry. I read a lot of Bukowski and Thoreau, transcendental guys. I grew up with hip-hop too, though, so every song got me into Tupac and Biggie and Pharcyde and Common. That era was so lyrical. We were hip-hop kids, and we're smarter than you think we are. Hip-hop is more than music and melody. Architecture, fashion, filmmaking, it's all part of it. Those are the street poets. Plus all the stuff that came with my parents— Bob Dylan, Cat Stevens, I loved them, too.

We're a remix culture. No one does just one thing. Poetry plays into people's lives in a way that might be bigger than they recognize. From how I see it, it's all poetry. My friends are poets, and we write scripts and books as well, because we don't want to wind up in one lane. But that's also the romantic in me, trying to see the poetry in the world.

Opening our own venue happened organically. I've always been someone with a wide network, and I'm proud of that community-building. I think it comes from my mom. Because I'm an actor, it's not like I'm working every day. In between gigs, there are months where you're trying to stay creative the whole time. To keep those muscles active. Got a camera, took pictures, started a band with my brother, and then a poetry venue. In a lot of ways, that's my college. That's my education. I also did it because we didn't know any better. But it worked out. Years later, it's still going strong.

Setting aside the time for poetry can be hard. Especially in 2019. Trying to stick to it is difficult. With National Poetry Month in April, I participated in the challenge to write a new poem every day. Small poems, just for me. I just finished writing a screenplay with my brothers for a small movie I'm directing this summer. I wrote in my journal about the city around me, and that's how I've always written. I'm at the age where all my friends are getting married, and they want me to read something at their weddings. So I do. Throughout the years, a few people have asked me to write a verse about their relationship, or the birth of a child.

Over the years, it's been easier to write for me. Process-wise, poetry always came pretty easily. Writing plays, writing screenplays, this book: it all starts with poetry for me. It's a compliment but also a lot of pressure, when people ask for a poem for their celebration. It's nerve-racking. It's a special occasion. One of my friends is a poet who got married, and I was like, "Damn, it's gonna be all poets at the wedding and I've gotta do a poem?" But there are events in my family where I'll want to mark the experience with a poem. The older we get, the more information we have to craft into art.

We all want to be eloquent, but ultimately, it's all emotions. Just feelings. I remember my first time feeling like a writer, during a junior high essay content. I wrote an essay on gangs, and then I won the contest. And had to read it in front of the school. And I had friends in gangs. But I read it to the end anyway, terrified. That was the first affirmation. Yet it's not just about sharing my poems, it's also about hearing other people's stories.

That's what the Poetry Lounge is about. Not any kind of elitism. We've done well, we've won poetry slams, but it's never been about that for me. I've had enough competition in my life as an artist. When I'm doing poetry, I don't want to race. It's just about getting on a mic and sharing your story. There's value in that connection.

When I was at Roni's Backstreet Poetry— I don't even know her name, but I remember her, I see her. This poet spoke about domestic abuse. A man, I assume her father, beat her mom. There was a simple line I'll never forget: "The color of the blood as it ran down the avocado-green refrigerator..." As a line, you're just in. You see it, you're there. That got me feeling poetry, and examining the details of my life much closer. Over the years, there's been a generation of poems that impacted me. I'd say every four or five years, a new era creates amazing poems, incredible poems.

Which begs the question: how do you judge who an up-and-comer is in poetry? How do you judge who might be a future champion in that scene, when it's so egalitarian? It's that balance. You'll come in and everyone's on the same mic. Everybody's good, but nobody's good. There's a balance. It's like comedy— to me, comics and poets are flip sides of the same coin. Poets try build a scene, same as comics. This is Hollywood, a town raised on stories. All of these comics are getting movies and specials and that's alright, but the poets— I want to get that platform for them. It takes some tweaking about how we get poets to do their sets and tell their stories. The studios need to see that their stories are just as adaptable as anything else, just as necessary for the world.

I'm a grown-up now, looking ahead at the future of our venue. I really want to find us our own home. A historical building to host our community, with classes on poetry several nights a week, performances, outreach programs. I want to solidify the Poetry Lounge in L.A.. Build a foundation for future writers from all walks of life. It's worth shooting for. Maybe you'll come out and help me? Or at least swing through, grab a seat, and spare us a snap.

BRIDGES TO THE BEYOND

About ten years ago, Mako passed away.

Mako Iwamatsu, one of the biggest, most prolific Asian artists in America for the past 40 years. In theatre, film, and voice-over. He played played my uncle several times over my career, and he was always a sageful voice in my life. He'd check with me while we were working, like, "What are you doing, what's going on?" We worked together for the first time when I was 12, in a movie called *The Perfect Weapon*. Mako really saw me grow up, and it was an honor working with him every single time, because Mako was a true uncle to me, and to the community at large. He created East West Players, the longest-running theater for Asian Americans. I grew up in that theater.

I was there when he passed away.

In his death, he continues to teach me. He's part of this lineage of excellent Asian performers from around the world. I strive to be part of that lineage, too. That's one of the other things he taught me: it's not only about you in your career.

He taught me that you have to give to the next generation. So I started creating films.

Alongside A.J. Rafael, I created an Asian American arts coalition called We Own The 8th, which celebrated Asian American arts on the 8th of every month. It's not enough to celebrate Asian American Month—which, by the way, no one even knows what month it is, including Asians. We figured, why can't we celebrate our media the eighth day of *every* month? Eight is a lucky number for tons of Asian cultures. I still remember the first meeting. A handful of my friends on the traditional media side: actors, directors, producers, folks like that. Then about a dozen big YouTubers at the time. We started having these conversations, like, "Where are we at? Where do we want to be?"

It was a State of the Union for Asian representation.

The conversation kept going for four years, every eighth of every month. It went from twenty or so people to over a hundred people a month. We screened short films from local filmmakers, and hosted live performances from singer-songwriters. We brought in keynote speakers, like my talks with John Chu, the director of *Crazy Rich Asians*, about what our stories mean beyond ourselves. Monthly, we could all take back the narrative of what it means to Asian in American, and educate the next generation of content creators out there. Of course, everyone wants their own careers to scale, but at the same time, your win is everyone's win. Everyone's win means something right here, right now.

The group closed after four years, as A.J. and I both had to focus on our work, but the energy lives on as those artists continue to collaborate. It still is a very cool moment right now for Asian artists, because everyone's rooting for and supporting each other. That group was part of the catalyst for me, to write and produce Asian American films.

When we talk about Asian media, people might wonder why it's so important.

Ninety percent of the roles in Hollywood are from the perspective of a white man. I'm not saying it's a false perspective, I'm saying that it's his reality of the world. The universe is much larger than that. According to UCLA's Hollywood Diversity Report of 2019, less than one out of ten film writers are people of color. Going forward with new media, it can't be imbalanced like that. We have to be the leader of our own stories

We know that when we watch movies, we're walking in the shoes of the hero. We've walked in the shoes of white men forever. We've saved the world, and fallen in love through their eyes. We know them very well. But everyone deserves a stage. So we create media with more truthful stories, from our own points of view. That's the mission.

My generation believed we would inherit the world, but the world changed. Biggest change since the Baby Boomers. Now it's for the generation beneath us. And they've certainly earned it. I'm working for people younger than I am.

Some people from my generation are upset about that. But I don't agree. I think our generation is the bridge, because the kids today move so fast and communicate so quickly that the rest of us can only try to catch up. That puts them in a very powerful position. On the other hand, there are still aspects of the industry that haven't changed since talkies were an innovation. These bridges need to be built, the communication must go both ways.

That's my role now. To be the bridge. I couldn't be happier.

What we began ten years ago, making Asian American films, grew into the movement for New Asian Media. I want to cultivate our slice of the American pie. As Asians, we're six percent of the population. Whoever we are, I want to cultivate us. I want us to be the arbiters of taste for our own stories. It's small, but we should be given our slice. If you aren't given your slice, kids, then carve it. Carve it out and dare them to take it back.

Then I was enlightened by other thinkers who told me I was thinking too small. "You're talking about the pie in America, let's look at the world: we are the pie." New Asian Media is us pivoting from America to the world. It's about tapping into what Asian countries have been doing for years. I'm a student of international cinema stretching back decades, as well as the latest TikTok.

It's easy for an older guy to say the new generation is selfish or whatever, but there's good and bad in everything. When we were kids, we competed with the people we knew. That was hard enough for our generation. Now kids size themselves up against the world. How can I be the cool kid in school when there's another kid in another school who has 30,000 followers on Instagram? There's an anxious self-awareness built into their lives. And that awareness mimics the scale and challenge I faced moving to LA after being a hometown hero. It's scary, and not reacting to it with absolute poise, as a child, seems like something we should forgive more easily.

The place where you can see the bridge the clearest? It's from a story. That's what I do. The kids spending hours editing their own videos, putting together projects with their friends— they're all storytellers, too. It's remarkable and strange. It's all of that rolled into one.

I've traveled back and forth to the Philippines for the last decade or so, working, shooting projects, and I've been involved in the arts scene out there, both firsthand and through my artist friends. I got to witness an incredible scene, of movie stars and fashion designers and directors. As a Filipino American, I wondered why we don't have this platform in America. I feel called to help even the playing field for Asian American artists, Filipino artists in particular. And I realized, there are actors and performers around the world, creating art on high levels, making fortunes; all the style and substance is there—how can we create this here in Hollywood? I know that doing the little bit roles that Hollywood throws out for Asians is not enough. I know that 99% of our roles we've seen since the birth of Hollywood over a hundred years ago, have been a white man's definition of Asian, often strewn with racism. It's not the whole story, not by a long shot. It's time for us to produce our own experiences, telling our own stories.

My time in the Philippines encouraged me to partner with James Sereno in Kinetic Films, an Asian American Pacific Islander film company coming out of Hawaii. So far we've been able to produce three films: *Paradise Broken*, *Hang Loose*, and *Man Up*.

When I went to Hawaii for the first time, I found a kind of liberation I've never known on the mainland. We're the majority, and so many barriers that shut us out in other parts of the country just don't exist there. Every store, every restaurant, everything you go into is run by Asian Pacific Islanders. It was so enlightening.

So I started putting up projects out in Hawaii with James; instead of one movie, it's a slate of films. When you produce films, you're able to employ so many people, whether they're in front of the camera or behind. It's a training ground. You can only get better at making movies...by making movies. This generation of artists needs practice as much as they need support for their own projects.

People ask how you employ a whole film set, and ensure that representation exists throughout. Luckily, when I hooked up with James, he had his whole system already built in Hawaii from doing commercials. So we just blew that system up to make films. It's not shooting one commercial over a week, it's shooting four commercials over four weeks. And instead of four commercials, it's a movie. He had a stable of really fine Asian American directors and DPs and editors. Like I said, when you go to Hawaii, it's predominantly Asian-Pacific Islander, so all the work that Hollywood does? They do the same in Hawaii. It's about us creating, and inspiring others to create films. Can we spark a fire to warm the artists than come after us?

The first project focused on getting representation with the leads. Our first film was called *Hang Loose*, starring me and Kevin Wu, and it was a Hangover-meets-Swingers kind of thing. If you don't capture the comedy side of it—if you're doing text-book safe representation, then why should anyone care? What does it preserve? So we got some writers together: myself, Kev, a dude named Benjamin Arthur— talented actor/comedian guy from Canada who'd won a bunch of awards, and who we talked into writing with us. We didn't know what we were doing, and we still don't. But little by little, we have to make it. It's like a *Field Of Dreams* thing: build it, and they will come. Hopefully.

We did three films in Hawaii, then things took off. You-Tube hit, with Asian American faces behind the wave—A.J. Rafael, Ryan Higa, Tim DeLaGhetto—these guys have real-ly stuck together. Along with all the fans who just see them as entertainment, there's a big Asian audience, so excited to see somebody who looks like them on-screen. That joy was really the impetus that got me into the whole scene. I'm old enough to understand how the traditional media world runs, and young enough to know how to use Twitter to con-nect with folks. It's a really sweet spot for me, to make these films and befriend the new kids as I learn from them.

We're creating a galaxy in the U.S. with stars in film, tele-vision, and online, but it's still really small. Singapore, China,

Japan, India— these industries all have massive stars, with so many projects and so much support. It's time for us to build that bridge, and bring Asian American talent into Asia, and welcome Asians stars to the industry out here. That's this new Asian media initiative that we're building towards. Ultimately, borderless Asian media. It's all ideas, you know? As an artist, you get passionate about an idea, and no one really tells you to do it. You have to give permission to yourself to dream.

I'm trying to raise money and the producers say, "Are you crazy? Why don't we just put a white person in this role, to sell more tickets?" I'm like, "No, no, there's a reason why we're doing this. It means something when it's an Asian lead." That's what we're trying to do. Two years later, I'm talking to people to fund projects and they're like, "Hey, you were right. I didn't see it coming, but you knew something I didn't." It's why I'm so thankful to *Crazy Rich Asians* and that whole crew for helping to capture what's possible.

The human experience is the human experience. We're having this conversation on the screen, in the movies. The funny movies, the historic films, the dramas. They all exist.

We shouldn't pigeonhole ourselves. We've been pigeonholed by Hollywood long enough.

Hollywood just happens to be the center of pop culture, and it just happens to be in America. It happens to be predominantly white people doing it. So in this era, where the mainstream is starting to recognize the full diversity of the world, you can't have white people doing "us." They don't know us. We must describe our views from our own perspective. Consequently, there will be white people in our projects from *our perspective*.

That's the conversation of art. We haven't had enough of our voices in the conversation to really impact. That's the conversation; we are all making movies. You're going to see my perception of you at times, which you may or may not like.

We're all human at the end of the day, and humans are inherently social. The essence of people is humanistic. We've seen ourselves in white people this whole time. When you make movies, the audience becomes the protagonist, which almost always happens to be a white man. We have all walked in the footsteps of a white male. We can explain all the idiosyncrasies and quirks, and maybe that's beautiful, but Black, Latinx, Asian, and Indigenous folks? We're not gifted the same consideration, the same empathy. The audience doesn't walk in our shoes nearly as often.

A lifetime watching the world through the lens of whiteness can change you. But then again, things change. I grew up in a predominantly Black and Latinx neighborhood. I worked in Hollywood, which is predominantly white. Where do I fit in? There were no roles for a Filipino guy, but I've been able to work for over thirty years. Somehow, my humanity shone through. But I've also been aware of my race my whole life. Will white people ever be as conscious? Will they give up power to do that? They should.

It's inevitable. If guided by good art, my hope is that they will. That's the beauty of art. It resonates with everyone. It has universal truth. I have faith in this generation to lead the conversation; they're always on the next stuff. You talk to my nieces and nephews and the younger kids, they seem decades wiser than me at that age.

All this builds to a sort of natural bottleneck, a question: Do I resent white people? Do I resent white culture for looming large over my entire career, but also over everyone I know? Every aspect of our lives?

This town has been good to me. That's not the most progressive answer, but I've seen the good in people at all times and in all places. Obviously not everyone is pure of heart, but as the guy who got to push so many boundaries, I've seen how good these folks have been at letting the standards change. I think I've seen more effort put into changing the boundaries in my career than I've seen people fighting on behalf of the status quo.

I'm worried about the world, because we're in a really crazy place. I'm hopeful, because you can't have change without growing pains. Real change doesn't happen without pain and conflict. My hope is that this misery will lead us to actual revolution. As far as resentment, I've never functioned that way. My goal is always to stay connected, and not get lost in all the shiny things. I was around a community of artists that didn't have the good fortune that I've had in this industry. Some members of that community were some of the closest people to me, I can never just ignorantly agree that it's all good. It's fine, but there's room for improvement.

Here's what I offer up to everyone, of every background, hoping to turn this industry inside out:

Ultimately, you're dealing with people who have their own agendas, and that's all valid. But you can encourage the process overall, and inspire people to do something that's beyond them. It's hard to get companies to invest in something they're probably going to lose money on initially, you know? But how do you get a company to do that anyway?

First of all, you collaborate with people who have similar agendas, and experience, to your own. Working horizontally with your local community. Other people like myself have less to lose, because they've already established themselves artistically or financially. Then it's literally selling dreams. Which is easier now since the new generation is so much more woke than mine; that's part of the conflict right now. These young people see how things can be better, and it's a matter of appealing to that instinct in the rest of us. And at the end of the day, it's getting a group of really hardcore workers to produce a final draft. You can't even begin to think about winning if you haven't made anything. Even making one thing is just a lottery ticket. How will you win?

I've made indie films in LA where I've asked everyone on the crew to believe in what we're doing and take pay cuts, and they did. In Hawaii, I'm working with a commercial team but I'm asking some of them to do the same in service of what we hope to create later. Like I said, we're in a moment where *Crazy Rich Asians* really captured the imagination of what's possible.

If an indie company, by some grace of the gods, puts out one film a year, as opposed to one film every five years, then that's progress. That's great, but that's not enough. If they want to scale— we've learned from the YouTube community that creators can consistently make content and earn revenue. They keep winning over the next generation, and it's just as viable as this billion-dollar studio. In some cases, more viable. That's the game changer. You don't want to do all cheap films and burn out a community, but you also want to let the community know that it's on us to make these movies. Going to a predominantly white studio to make content for people of color has been and will always be part of the strategy in trying to get something made, but now it's not the only strategy. We can fund our work from the top and build from the bottom. We keep making films and busting our asses, but the next round is going to be a little bit better.

The worst thing you could do is approach a rich white person and ask if they want to fund the next *Crazy Rich Asians*. To have their name on something that would prove how progressive and diverse they are. Oh no. I hope no one tries that.

I want to stick with the math. I'd go, "You can do one film for two million dollars in one shot. But I say give me two million dollars, I'll put a production group together and make ten films for $200,000 apiece." A two million dollar film is a long shot in Hollywood, anyway. So might as well have ten long shots. One of these young artists might be the next Spielberg, we don't know yet.

This all goes back to Mako. He passed on. Afterwards, I felt like I picked up the torch. Not just for the art that we were making, but for representation. If he were here now I think he'd be pushing on the culture the way that I'm constantly prodding it to be better.

At the time I was in my mid-thirties, and questioning who I was. What I stood for.

The industry often feeds the most selfish parts of ourselves. For better or worse, hustling your own rising star can be very isolating. There are moments where you're like, "Is this all about me?" That doesn't sit well with me, so it's necessary to do something for others. That's far more rewarding.

There's an inverse possibility here. You step back, and you spend all of your time fostering new voices. But then you miss out on jobs. And you miss out on jobs because white actors who take time to mentor… they don't lose out on momentum. That just becomes something they do on the side. If I stop pushing the Dante career out there, I'll fade. And if I fade, would I become resentful of the new voices? Or resentful of how racism has held me back from being the multi-faceted artist that I know myself to be?

It's almost a volition. Acting itself is volition, a matter of willpower. The fact that you're even here doing it means that we're travelers. The majority of people in Hollywood have gotten in a damn car or train, and came here from somewhere else. They're on their own hero's journey. They left wherever the hell they're from, and bet on themselves When you're in a bar and there's a bunch of drunken heroes on their hero's journey, anything can happen on any night. We're a town of deviants and misfits, dealing with damage. Sometimes that hurt makes the town so dope. It's like we tell artists: it's going to fuck you up, but lean into it. Everyone's in their own process that we don't know about.

I get excited about who we are, each of us as humans. You deal with everybody for who they are. One of the things that keeps me alive is I'm insatiably inquisitive. Everything's still a wonder to me. It could be a YouTuber and how big his impact is, or it could be interviewing a plumber to research a new character. That's the great thing about acting: we don't have a real job; our job is to see what other people do, and why their lives are so interesting.

Our job is to study the human condition, and the human condition is more than just the good stuff.

For my friends, my life can be difficult to parse. As much time as I spend trying to avoid the spotlight, I spend more time attending conventions and festivals, very much under the glare of attention. It's a relationship with the audience, with the fans. Sometimes, I must re-examine my relationship there. As many performers must in this age of direct fan access. But there are some basic standards. You know: don't be a dick. Don't be a predator. The decencies that should be easy, but some people apparently choose to ignore.

I try to find out why fans like my work, what makes it so interesting. To an extent, your audience informs what you do. What's wild is that the world's changed so much that people say, "I like the stuff you do, but I'm really a fan of how you deal with fans, and the way you think." I'm like "What?" This is a whole other level of entertainment. That's crazy. Different responsibility. I appreciate it, but everyone has their own perspective of everything. Everyone's living in their own movie. It's not so much you, but what you reflect in them.

People come up and tell me about how invested they are in my life. That can be difficult to sort out, when I might assume that me and that person probably have nothing else in common. But even then, that's never fully true. You're only a fan of artists because they reflect you, on some level. That's how it goes. That's empowering as artists, because we're able to connect with people.

The other side of it is that for my entire adult life, people have approached me to describe what kind of impact my characters had on their lives. Sometimes it's small, and sometimes a movie helped them meet their spouse. None of this, of course, ever comes from a negative place, but some folks might be more conscious than others. People just grab you and shout a feeling at you. Perhaps I'm dealing with a difficult break-up, and I'm just trying to find the restroom. Then this happens.

I promise I'm not complaining, but it can be a tricky balance to maintain.

I live at conventions now, and that defines such a chunk of my life. It's a lot of darting between the public and the private side of things. Not just on the show floor, but just making it back to my hotel room without creating an uncomfortable situation. And my worst fear, obviously, is that someone will catch me. Catch me in a human moment where I'm processing something they could not possibly be aware of, and then I do something that will always make them think, "Wow, that Dante sure sucks." No one remembers that you're in a human position with the random nature of human problems. I don't blame them, because especially on the show floor, I forget about it too.

Did you know that a break-up can come at any time?

It can. It's not on the people that are excited to see you. But it's impossible to fill them in as to why you're not up to taking a Bangarang selfie with them at that exact moment.

These are just the kind of things that wind up on your emotional plate. Overwhelmingly, the experience of every social crossover leaves both me (and I hope the people I interact with) in a place of brutal positivity that bleeds over into the next day. We all have battle scars and we all have hindrances, but there's a regenerative element in the con world. We feed off each other. I don't always know what state fans are in, but when one shares a tale of overcoming adversity with me, that fuels my next week as I dive into the next project, which I hope will replicate that experience.

Conventions are also a chance for me to see everyone I came up with in the industry. It's a tight group of Hollywood survivors. We all made it. Even those of us with a single cult credit, we all found what we were looking for. And we aren't dead. That sounds bleak but I assure you that I find a reason to celebrate. Considering all of those friends I've lost.

Maybe that feels weird to read. I get it. I spend so much of my nights worrying that I've become a fraud. What I tell young artists is that you can't take anything personal. It is advice that I should take to heart more often.

I have this approach to when those moments of negativity arise, especially from social media. I believe that we should take our licks and keep on ticking. I can hear you shouting at me right now, dear reader. Yes, that's a stupid middle child philosophy to have. But I'm a middle child. Come at me, bro. Genuinely, that kind of criticism will only matter after you've interrogated the source. If the person means a lot to you, then of course it can hit you hard. If this is from a stranger from nowhere, let them slide off into infinite space. Question yourself and your motives, but also know when someone has painted you as a cartoon, and ignore it.

As a quick aside: social media makes me feel doomed most days, like we as a society missed the whole point of everything. It's bizarre. I look to the new generation for hope, because they're more evolved, but at the same time, I'm scared. From politics to climate change, these issues can either destroy us all or blossom into true change. We have to work for the world we want, it's not a foregone conclusion that we'll end up in the right place. If you can add to the collective hope, then that's beautiful.

I don't know what to do if someone approached me at a con and says they're a fan, but they're wearing a MAGA hat. I'm thrilled to be the kid you know from a movie in the 90s, but if you stand against the oppressed, you stand against me. It's hard; I'm a person of color, you're going to come and take a picture with me? What are you doing? Make America Great Again? The world rotates every day. The ever-evolving human is going to evolve. There's no going back. To go back to something that was supposedly better? I don't believe that's evolution.

I think it all boils down to empathy, through helping those people to see the world beyond themselves. We're going to come to a head, certainly. I can only do it through art.

You've got to fight however you can, impact the way you can impact. We'll have to figure out the rest. I hope that I live atop a wave of positive communal experience that can show some faint glimmer of joy to the worst of humanity. If they refuse to see, then we have to stand up for what we believe in.

As an artist, I'm always thinking about what's next. It's nice to look back to celebrate my accomplishments, but ultimately, it's all about staying creative. So next for me is: the book's coming out, I've become partners in a new company called The

Machine with Rawn Erickson, and I'm directing a movie, my first time directing this year. My compass, the hope that guides me, is to create opportunities for the next generation. I'm trying to create this bridge between the U.S. and the Philippines, and help support artists in both. In so many ways, Uncle Mako led me.

When he passed, I was in my thirties. I work to be part of his lineage, and create space for the time after me. The opportunities and ability to reinvent yourself as an actor never change. There are more mountains to climb. But there's this urge to make it better for the next generation. The people before us made it better for us, and we must do the same.

ADVICE AND ADIEU

I've written a lot about myself. You might be sick of me by this point. I have a lot of thoughts, and a lot of stories and, for the time being, I think we've exhausted the big ones. I'll certainly have more by the time we do the next book. (Does that read like a veiled threat? Possibly.)

Before closing out what I've shared in these pages, I'd like to distill some of those stories into their most useful form as direct advice. For actors, artists, poets, and perhaps just you as a person. I want to have a chapter here that provides the clearest version of everything I've learned in my time in this industry, and what my forty-plus years of life have gifted me.

I'm a journeyman actor. A blue-collar actor. I'm just a guy who does his job, when he has a job to do. I don't make millions of dollars, despite working at this for several decades. I'm often surprised that I've survived in this haphazard business. At the end of every year, I take a long exhale and thank the powers that be. That I'm here. For another year. That I'm getting to make a living doing what I enjoy. That I get to be creative as a career.

When talking of Hollywood success, many talk about luck. And yes, luck is at the core of overcoming the astronomical odds of what we're up against. It's also ridiculously dismissive of the work that goes into this. It sucks to hear when you're in the middle of the work. Obviously, that labor doesn't guarantee that an artist will find success. In a way, that's the fun of it. You gamble. Not just with your life as a whole, but with every new project that you attempt. Or every relationship you form. Or every skill you add to your bag of tricks. There's always the potential of striking it rich. More often, you'll strike out. And you could keep striking out forever. It's a real lottery ticket purchase of a career. That means you'll have to establish structures to make sure all these choices reward you as a person. You need to make sure you take care of yourself, and keep your head above water.

Keep that in mind when you see someone make it big, and you know in your heart of hearts that your skill eclipses theirs. Use that to further your dedication, but never become resentful. Negativity will never help you get to where you're going, but that doesn't mean that a little spark of revenge won't light a fire.

Getting good is nothing short of hard work. You do the work and you make your luck. I studied for 20 years in a conservatory, and plenty of people studied alongside me that went nowhere. They were no less brilliant at the craft. That's the lottery. Getting good is no luck at all. That's the job.

There are so many bad movies out there. There are so many good movies out there. There are so many actors with incredible talent, and even more incredible missteps. There are people that stumbled into success and there are those that spent a lifetime climbing the ladder to get there.

Don't let anyone ever tell you that it's just luck. There will always be variables, a set of systems outside of your control. Occasionally, these variables will seem stacked against you. But you, with a good head on your shoulders and a work ethic to match… you will always be the constant. If you believe enough, there is nothing that can stand in your way forever.

That's the luck.

"Seek out and study with a master

If you're after

Greatness

The aim is

Impact the world & be a catalyst for changes

Forget what your name is

You should want to be good

More than you want to be famous."

Write about what you know, write about what you see. If you're trying your material out in the world, don't go on too long during open mics. Not everyone will find your poems or jokes as fascinating as you might find them. It's better to leave people wanting more, than for people to want you to leave. Remember a poem is a story with a beginning, a middle and an end, even if it's just one line long. If you felt the urge to write about it, you should write about it. Your story matters. Don't indulge yourself too much, basking in the sound of your voice speaking your words. A performance is communication, not masturbation.

This business is about people working with people. When

choosing an agent or manager, find someone that really gets you and you get them. It's a relationship, like picking someone to date... it can last years and be more like a marriage!

Fame is just a tool. It will open some doors for you, sweeten some deals, and could help create more opportunities for you but in and of itself it's like smoke. It can be really dense and heavy, but it can also just disappear.

You're not as bad as anyone will ever say you are, but you're also not as good either. You're just you. Modulate that expectation. If you put too much weight on the likes and applause, the negative stuff will hit you on the backswing. When you do a play, you work your ass off for two hours on stage, and the audience applauds for a few minutes at the end. Concentrate on the two hours of work. And remember the limitations of a single ovation. Prep yourself and have some expectations of both the amount of work you're putting in, and the amount of response you'll get back.

The last big thing to hit on before we say adieu for now, is a final thought on art.

This book contains a number of stories about dedication to the form, and about my journey to get there. In Hollywood, you'll wind up getting hurt. That's true of any pursuit in any city, especially as an artist. That gamble takes a toll. What we encounter is having to open ourselves up to let all the Good out. The Bad will use this opportunity to get in. A horrifying number of opportunists might try to take advantage of you in this state. That will always— and trust me, the hurt never changes— that will always suck.

Every artist I admire carries their damage, and uses it. That never ceases to impress me. Not that they need the hurt to make a good thing, but that they can process it. Make it count. Make it inspire others. Shape it into a completely different beast.

I believe that you need to open up enough to be vulnerable, because you need that exposure to make art. If you get hurt, find a way to convert it into art, but don't go out looking for hurt. Not every great artist needs to survive trauma, and if you feel like you're stuck in a rut, do not seek choices that will hurt you.

We'll all human, with the capacity to be harmed. We will to bruise and suffer and cry, and react poorly, and scare people away. That's part of it. But never believe that you require that hurt as a constant to fuel what you are.

You're stuck with the character and the character is stuck with you. Simply meaning, work on the character, work on yourself. The character that you play is trapped within the confines of you, so if you work on yourself you can expand the boundaries of the characters you play.

It's ironic that as an actor, there's often a misconception that we are just good liars in make-believe worlds. Actually, we succeed as actors when we've uncovered some truth in a character or story, and can communicate it to you. When our truth resonates with yours, it impacts all of our worlds.

I've spent my career leaning into pain, and hoping that I can spin it into gold. Let's be honest: I would've preferred to reach those places without the underlying Suck. And between that and general self-care, there's no reason to hunt it down. I see so much performative pain in the creative field. People who believe they'll be taken more seriously if it seems like they're always miserable, if they constantly call your attention to how hard they punish themselves over their art. People who go Method and never come back from it. A few of them are very successful but, let's be real here, no one wants to be around that in the long-term.

If you're vulnerable, be prepared to take some losses and carry some shit with you because of that. Don't fake it. Don't live in it for no reason. Only fake artists pretend their way through art, and that's because they don't have anything genuine to offer.

Ultimately, your honest losses are badges of honor. Things like not talking to my family for years and not being the person you want to be— those aren't choices I'm proud of. Talking about it in this book is very— sigh. Sigh is what I have to say. But it's real. No one's perfect. There a cost of admission for everything. It happened to me. You can blame anything for why this or that may or may not have happened in your career. That might be true, but your career keeps going, and the next thing you make may be better than anything you could've gotten before. It's just life.

Don't torture yourself in pursuit of forcing art to happen. But life is what life is, and you'll find power that comes from your lowest moments. Take the good; leave the bad.

Take care of yourself, reader, above all. Nothing is worth more than you. Especially now, when the world appears to always be moments from bursting into flames. We can only control ourselves.

When it goes poorly, find your path through.

For me, it's art. I can always write a poem, I can always audition for the next job. Go work. Do a play. Power, money, other relationships, expectations from others: these can all cloud your judgment. You can find yourself in a hole as I have, and the only way out of it is to out-produce the negativity by creating. Create for yourself. Write a story, an essay, a poem, go to an open mic, make a movie on your damn iPhone. What brought you joy? Start doing that again. You'll find clarity. The things that gravitate towards you will be the right things. Take the experiences you've had thus far to a new level next time. Resilience can be even more important than pure creativity.

That's my way through. You do what you need to do. I'm a workaholic, but maybe you need to completely disconnect and go sit in a park. It's all valid.

Just as significant as taking care of yourself is knowing when you need to do so.

I couldn't sleep because of racing thoughts, because of depression. There's a broken engagement I mentioned in the beginning of this book. We're still friends, we've got a lot of love for each other, but there's still dealing with failure.

So I went to therapy.

I'm Filipino. Ethnic people are not really keen on therapy. I had to find a way to forgive myself. I'm never fully over anything, it's a day-to-day struggle. Half the time, I'm flying around the world doing conventions and shooting projects. I've had friends say, "Hey man, you're running away from life."

Maybe. But I'm trying to use some of that energy to create something. I'm not sitting here waiting for it to come get me. It's going to get you. It has gotten me; I've had to face myself before. I'd just rather do it in a hotel room while shooting a project than on my own. It just hits me during a layover. I need time to process my thoughts.

Writing remains a really good place for me to anchor those racing thoughts. It's hard for some people. Some people don't think the life they're living is even worth writing about. I have the luxury and arrogance where, at least to me, it matters. My voice matters, even if it just matters to me. I won't live my life without confronting myself. I can't do that. I have to look at myself, and what I've done.

Find a way to engage in the conversations you want to engage in, and you can do artistic work the way you want to. We're either the lucky ones or the cursed ones for having a bigger appetite for creativity. But at the end of the day, that's what we do. You want to be a jack of all trades on a film set, you want to be involved in every department. I'm not a master of anything, but I have something to add to any project: my vision. And beyond the great work we want to leave behind, don't forget the greatest piece of art should be the life you live.

I'm not doing it to show people how great I am. I just want to tell my stories.

If you have a story, you'll find a way to tell it. Take care along the way.

From me to you, thank you for reading this. And good luck on the journey. Or, whatever luck you make for yourself. You know what that means.

-Dante Basco

About the Author

With a career spanning over three decades, **Dante Basco** is a Hollywood actor who has become a cult classic and pioneering figure in Asian American cinema. He was first introduced in Steven Spielberg's fairytale movie *Hook*, as "Rufio", the leader of the Lost Boys. He continued working in films with leading roles like Newline's *Take the Lead*, opposite Antonio Banderas, and starring in *The Debut*, which became the voice of a Filipino American generation. 20th Century Fox executives were so mesmerized by the uniqueness of Dante's look and ability that they gave him a development deal for his own series and he starred in a pilot for Touchstone/ABC, *The Chang Family Saves the World,* written and produced by John Ridley and directed by Paris Barclay. Ever versatile, he's "Jake Long" in Disney's animated series *American Dragon: Jake Long* as well as "Prince Zuko" in Nickelodeon's phenomenal hit, *Avatar: The Last Airbender.*